SpringerBriefs in Criminology

Policing

Series editor

M.R. Haberfeld
City University of New York
John Jay College of Criminal Justice
New York, NY, USA

More information about this series at http://www.springer.com/series/11179

James C. Brown · Raymond L. Philo
Anthony Callisto Jr. · Polly J. Smith

Command Transitions in Public Administration

A Quantitative and Qualitative Analysis of Proactive Strategies

Springer

James C. Brown
Department of Economic Crime
and Justice Studies
School of Business and Justice Studies
Utica College
Utica, NY
USA

Anthony Callisto Jr.
Division of Campus Safety
and Emergency Services
Syracuse University
Syracuse, NY
USA

Raymond L. Philo
Department of Economic Crime
and Justice Studies
School of Business and Justice Studies
Utica College
Utica, NY
USA

Polly J. Smith
Department of Sociology
School of Arts and Sciences
Utica College
Utica, NY
USA

ISSN 2192-8533 ISSN 2192-8541 (electronic)
SpringerBriefs in Criminology
ISSN 2194-6213 ISSN 2194-6221 (electronic)
SpringerBriefs in Policing
ISBN 978-3-319-27843-8 ISBN 978-3-319-27844-5 (eBook)
DOI 10.1007/978-3-319-27844-5

Library of Congress Control Number: 2015960820

Printed on acid-free paper

This Springer imprint is published by SpringerNature
The registered company is Springer International Publishing AG Switzerland

Contents

About the Authors

James C. Brown is an assistant professor of Criminal Justice in the School of Business and Justice Studies, joining the full-time faculty in January of 2014 after serving multiple senior administrative roles at Utica College, Utica, New York, since 2005. Most recently, Dr. Brown served as the vice president for the School of Online and Extended Studies and an adjunct instructor in the School of Arts and Sciences and School of Business and Justice Studies at Utica College. Dr. Brown also served as an assistant vice president for Marketing and Communications, assistant vice president for Academic Affairs and Dean of the School of Graduate and Extended Studies, and vice president for Strategic Initiatives.

Dr. Brown holds a bachelor's degree in criminal justice from Utica College (1988), a master's degree in public administration from Sage Graduate School in Albany (1994), where he was awarded the Outstanding Public Administration Student, and a doctorate in education from the University of Phoenix School of Advanced Studies in educational leadership (2007).

Dr. Brown's diverse background includes a 16-year full- and part-time career as a police officer, police commander, and police administrator, serving as Oneida County NY's first and youngest-ever Chief Deputy of Operations with the Oneida County Sheriff's Office. Dr. Brown also served as a police officer and Assistant Chief of Police for the Village of Frankfort, NY, and the City of Sherrill, NY. Dr. Brown also served as the Oneida County STOP-DWI Program Administrator for eight years and as a vice president for public relations, security, and facilities for the former Herkimer County Trust.

In 1996, he served as a volunteer police supervisor for the Security Team Program at the Centennial Olympic Games in Atlanta, Georgia, responsible for security at the Rhythmic Gymnastics, Volleyball, and Olympic Village at the University Georgia at Athens (UGA). Although unable to attend during the Games period, Dr. Brown was also selected as a member of the volunteer police force for the Utah Public Safety Command during the 2002 Winter Olympic Games in Salt Lake City, Utah.

Most recently Dr. Brown was sworn in as a Police Commissioner/Member and Deputy Chairman and Secretary of the New Hartford, NY Police Commission in January of 2014, having been duly appointed by the Town Board, and reappointed to a five-year term in January of 2015. Dr. Brown also served as the chairman of the transition team for Oneida County Sheriff Robert M. Maciol, leading the team responsible for preparing then Sheriff-Elect Maciol to recruit and select his senior management team and prepare all related aspects of assuming the office of the Sheriff on January 1, 2011.

Dr. Brown actively teaches on ground and online in the areas of Criminal Justice and Public administration. Dr. Brown is a member of the Academy of Criminal Justice Sciences (ACJS) and the Northeastern Association of Criminal Justice Sciences, as well as a Fellow with the Criminal Justice Educators Association of New York State. Dr. Brown is also a member of the American Society of Public Administration (ASPA). He also serves as an active member of the International Association of Chiefs of Police (IACP) and New York State Association of Chiefs of Police (NYSACOP). He is also a proud associate member of the United States Marine Corps League. Dr. Brown resides in New Hartford, New York, with his wife and three children.

Raymond L. Philo is a professor of Practice in Criminal Justice at Utica College and is the Executive Director of the Economic Crime and Cybersecurity Institute. He also served as Director of Research for the Department of Economic Crime, Justice Studies and Cybersecurity at Utica College. Professor Philo has served as a faculty member at Utica College since 2001, teaching both at the undergraduate and at the graduate levels. Prior to joining Utica College, he served as a law enforcement administrator, retiring as Chief of Police for the New Hartford, NY Police Department. Professor Philo received his BA degree in Political Science from Utica College and a Master's Degree in Public Administration from Marist College.

He holds numerous state and federal certifications in law enforcement operations and management. Philo is currently a licensed consultant with the New York State Division of Criminal Justice Services and is a member of The Association of Certified Fraud Examiners and The International Association of Chiefs of Police. Professor Philo also serves as a member of the Supervisory Committee at First Source Federal Credit Union and serves on the Board of Directors at the Griffiss Institute.

Professor Philo has taught courses in Criminal Evidence, Modern Methods of Criminal Investigation, Criminalistics, Senior Seminar, Counterterrorism and Homeland Security, and the Graduate Capstone Course in the Economic Crime Management Program.

Anthony Callisto Jr. is the senior vice president for Safety and Chief Law Enforcement Officer for Syracuse University, leading law enforcement, security, fire safety, environmental health, emergency management, risk management and parking and transit services staff and functions at Syracuse University. He was the University's Chief of Public Safety from 2006 to 2014 and is a retired Chief Deputy for the Onondaga Sheriff's Office, having served as chief for ten of his twenty-five years with the Sheriff's Office.

He is a past president of the following organizations: The American Jail Association, the Central New York Association of Chiefs of Police, the University Hill Public Safety Association, and a Food Bank of Central New York. He is a police instructor as well as a criminal justice, conflict resolution and labor relations consultant.

He holds a BA in Criminal Justice from Columbia College and a MA in Public Administration from Syracuse University. He is also an adjunct professor of Criminal Justice at Columbia College, where he has taught undergraduate and graduate criminal justice course for the past fifteen years.

Polly J. Smith is the associate provost for online learning, the vice president for the school of online and extended studies, and the associate professor of sociology at Utica College, Utica, NY. Dr. Smith specializes in the use of GIS technology and is an active participant within the field of sociology. She has worked in depth on a variety of local and national projects via the Lewis Mumford Center for Comparative and Urban Regional Research formally located at the University of Albany.

She is currently expanding her research on military bases and their relationship to metropolitan level segregation, which involves not only spatial analysis (GIS and Geoda), but also US Census data from 1980 to 2000 as well as the IPUMS data collection. In addition, she is involved in research looking at the value of educational television and the impact of growing populations in the Catskill region. The latter stems from a collaborative work in progress evaluating the current position of New York State and the relationship between upstate and downstate in terms of both national trends and future development which will be published by SUNY Press in the Fall of 2007.

Professor Smith is also an active participant in the New York State Sociological Association, the Eastern Sociological Association, and the American Sociological Association attending annual meetings as well as presenting current research, serving as a session presider and working on undergraduate committees.

Dr. Smith holds a bachelor's degree from Utica College and her Ph.D. from the State University of New York at Albany.

Command Transitions in Public Administration: A Quantitative and Qualitative Analysis of Proactive Strategies

Abstract Effective transitions of power are essential to the smooth operation of any public administration organization, in particular a criminal justice agency. Prior research has shown generalized discussion surrounding agency *succession* planning. Transitions, however, are differentiated from succession planning within this research, along with the associated attitudes and behaviors of those engaged in both behaviors. The purpose of this study was to provide a quantitative and qualitative analysis of proactive management strategies for command transitions for criminal justice and other public administration civil service, appointed, and elected agency leaders as analyzed and reported by those members involved in such transitions, responding members of two New York State criminal justice associations representing criminal justice command-level staff. The results of this study show that for the overall purposive sample population (n = 205), a statistically significant correlation exists between having clear job expectations when entering a new supervisory position and the new supervisor's high levels of self-reported satisfaction and preparedness as they transitioned into their new command position. This study represents the first known analysis in the United States that yields a comprehensive, actionable, criminal justice Command Transition Matrix© tool based on sound quantitative and qualitative research, as well as a successfully implemented actual transition experience as a baseline reference.

Introduction

Ample literature exists across multiple disciplines and public and private sectors regarding both the importance of and steps to successful succession planning (Elkin et al. 2012; Rothwell 2010; Withrow 2003). This research study clearly distinguishes transition planning from succession planning. Carter (1986), as cited in Rothwell (2010), suggests that succession planning is:

> a means of identifying critical management positions, starting at the levels of project manager and supervisor and extending up to the highest position in the organization. Succession planning also describes management positions to provide maximum flexibility

J.C. Brown et al., *Command Transitions in Public Administration*,
SpringerBriefs in Policing, DOI 10.1007/978-3-319-27844-5_1

> in lateral management moves and to ensure that as individuals achieve greater seniority, their management skills will broaden and become more generalized in relation to total organizational objectives rather than to purely departmental objectives. (p. 6)

For criminal justice agencies, the literature suggests that similar plans must be in place in tandem with leadership development and related supervisory and management training within an agency or organization (Michelson 2006; Withrow 2003). Nowhere in the literature, however, does there exist a platform for the discussion and importance of the heretofore seemingly ministerial and undocumented act(s) associated with the actual transition of power from entry-level criminal justice or other public administration employees to the most senior elected or appointed agency heads.

Screening for levels of satisfaction and preparedness after promotion or appointment into a command role is not prevalent in the United States but is needed to provide leaders with an inventory of potential predictive characteristics which may improve these transitions of power (Brown 2007). The current research study might provide criminal justice and other public administration leaders with new insights with respect to recognizing the formal and informal transition factors that affect their employees and using this understanding to implement preventive, mitigating, and corrective measures toward the implementation of an effective codified transition matrix, thus yielding a more satisfied and more well-prepared supervisor.

The purpose of this quantitative cross-sectional survey research was to examine whether or not the presence or absence of a formal or informal transition process resulted in higher levels of employee job satisfaction and preparedness (dependent variables) of members at two New York State criminal justice associations and their self-reported perceptions of job satisfaction and preparedness after promotion or appointment into a command role. The research methodology was quantitative, using a cross-sectional survey design to collect and analyze "data at one point in time" (Brown 2007; Creswell 2005, p. 355), primarily because of time limitations and the financial commitment that a longitudinal study would involve. Qualitative data were also collected in the form of open-ended questions to capture expanded responses of survey participants.

There are limitations associated with generalizing data produced by qualitative studies and the target population size; therefore, a quantitative approach was selected. Furthermore, the quantitative approach allowed single-layer rather than multiple-layer data scrutiny of the data pool (Horn 2004).

Quantitative analysis "is an inquiry approach useful for describing trends and explaining the relationship among variables found in the literature" (Brown 2007; Creswell 2005, p. 597). The quantitative method of research tends to yield a final document marked by objectivity and a lack of researcher bias. Dube and Pare (2003) suggested, "In quantitative research, well-known standardized statistical analysis methods (e.g., analysis of variance or regression) have helped researchers confirm or disconfirm hypotheses" (¶ 67). The scholarly dispute regarding the choice of quantitative or qualitative measures did not go unnoticed, for example, by federal legislators when the No Child Left Behind (NCLB) Act of 2001, 2002 was enacted.

Measurement associated with the NCLB Act takes many forms, but quantitative measures are clearly seen as the federal government's new standard for program evaluation in the education-specific [and public administration] environment (Horn 2004). For the present study, there was an intention to provide greater objectivity to the area of study, specifically within the field of criminal justice and public administration leadership, and a quantitative cross-sectional survey design accomplished this goal. The literature suggested that while qualitative and other forms of measurement might have a place in research, the trend in educational research insofar as the federal government is concerned is to focus more heavily on the scientific rigor associated with quantitative research methods (Brown 2007; Dube and Pare 2003; Horn 2004).

Research Questions

Screening for levels of satisfaction and preparedness after promotion or appointment into a command role is not prevalent in the United States but is needed to provide leaders with an inventory of potential predictive characteristics which may improve these transitions of power (Brown 2007). The current research study might provide criminal justice and other public administration leaders with new insights with respect to recognizing the formal and informal transition factors that affect their employees and using this understanding to implement preventive, mitigating, and corrective measures toward the implementation of an effective codified transition matrix. The following research question(s) guided this research:

1. Does a formal transition process result in a higher level of satisfaction after promotion or appointment into a command role?
2. Does a formal transition process result in a higher sense of preparedness after promotion or appointment into a command role?
3. Does an informal transition process result in a higher level of satisfaction after promotion or appointment into a command role?
4. Does an informal transition process result in a higher sense of preparedness after promotion or appointment into a command role?

Assumptions

An assumption in scholarly research has the same meaning as in everyday use and refers to taking something for granted (Hughes and Tomkiewicz 1994). For the purpose of the current research, it was assumed that all participants would answer the questionnaire honestly. It was further assumed that all participants were fairly representative of current or former employees of criminal justice agencies in the United States, and New York State in particular, by virtue of membership screening apparatus for each association, preventing any non-criminal justice agency member participation in the research. Differences between criminal justice agencies and their respective responsibilities, such as police departments, sheriff's offices, correctional facilities, civil offices, and related operations, were assumed to exist as well.

Scope

The scope of the research included two New York State criminal justice agency associations. The potential pool of survey participants or the target population was approximately 1237 members between the two associations ($N = 1237$). It is believed that each association, with its respective membership characteristics, is representative of the universe of criminal justice command (supervisory) level personnel in the United States. The two associations chosen for the study are not specifically referred to in order to ensure participant confidentiality.

Both associations are located in New York State, and both have tightly restricted primary membership to supervisory/command-level personnel only. These associations were selected because of their relative similarities in organizational structure and because both association's organizational leadership gave permission for the administration of a survey to their respective membership.

Criminal justice agencies, organizations, and associations, like those selected for this study, are not unfamiliar with participating in a multitude of surveys for a wide range of purposes. Beyond some of the most common law enforcement surveys, such as the Uniform Crime Reports (UCR) produced by the Federal Bureau of Investigation (FBI), the US Department of Justice's Office of Justice Programs, Bureau of Justice Statistics (BJS) serves as the official legal repository "directed to collect and analyze statistical information concerning the operation of the criminal justice system at the federal, state, and local levels" (The Public Health and Welfare 2006). According to BJS (2014),

> 'Law enforcement' is the term that describes the individuals and agencies responsible for enforcing laws and maintaining public order and public safety. Law enforcement includes the prevention, detection, and investigation of crime and the apprehension and detention of individuals suspected of law violation. (¶ 1)

The population selected for the current research study, law enforcement supervisors, was similar to the general categories and subcategories identified by the US Bureau of Justice Statistics. While sampling error is a part of all research, efforts to maximize the generalizability of the study findings to the entire population of law enforcement supervisors in the United States were made by "hav[ing] a good sampling frame list, as large a sample from the population as possible [in light of survey constraints], …and rigorous administration procedures" (Creswell 2005, p. 360). In this research, the characteristics of the population to be studied were known and restricted by clearly identifiable membership characteristics known to the researchers.

Summary

The most recent census of state and local law enforcement agencies conducted by BJS indicates that in the United States, there are 765,000 sworn law enforcement officers across 17,985 state and local law enforcement agencies (U.S. Department of Justice 2011). Of the 1237 members of the population selected for this study, 205, or 16.6 %, responded to the survey. Screening for levels of satisfaction and preparedness after promotion or appointment into a command role is not prevalent in the United States but is needed to provide leaders with an inventory of potential predictive characteristics which may improve these transitions of power (Brown 2007). The current research study might provide criminal justice and other public administration leaders with new insights with respect to recognizing the formal and informal transition factors that affect their employees and using this understanding to implement preventive, mitigating, and corrective measures toward the implementation of an effective codified transition matrix.

Review of the Literature

As the legally charged federal agency "directed to collect and analyze statistical information concerning the operation of the criminal justice system at the federal, state, and local levels" (The Public Health and Welfare 2006), the US Bureau of Justice Statistics possesses both the personnel and financial resources to conduct a multitude of criminal justice-related research studies, both short term and longitudinal. Of the many sources housed in the BJS library, the Law Enforcement Management and Administrative Statistics Survey (LEMAS) contain data on law enforcement agencies and their personnel since 1987, including core characteristic data such as sworn and unsworn personnel, full-time versus part-time employees, male versus female, race, and related demographic information, at a quadrennial estimated administered cost in 2012 of $768,953 (U.S. Department of Justice 2011; U.S. General Services Administration 2012, p. 22). In the 2012 LEMAS Supporting Statement, the researchers suggested,

> Another limited perspective on law enforcement comes from surveys conducted by university professors and law enforcement professional associations (e.g., Police Executive Research Forum, International Association of Chiefs of Police). These surveys are typically conducted among only a small number of large law enforcement agencies and, even among this limited sample, have survey response rates that rarely exceed fifty percent. The appearance of objectivity in academic or professional surveys is reduced when survey responses are used to support advocacy positions of the survey sponsor or when the details of the survey instrument, data collection, and data analysis are not publicly available for independent review. (U.S. General Services Administration 2012, p. 4)

This research study had a response rate of 16.6 %, dispersed across 205 New York State-based criminal justice commanders that supervise between 1 and 5500 sworn and civilian personnel. This research study is differentiated from LEMAS and related BJS studies in its attempt to more deeply analyze supervisor satisfaction and preparedness in the context of heretofore undocumented transitions of law enforcement personnel as they move from frontline criminal justice personnel into supervisory roles. The contributions of academic and related research work should be in tandem with and not in opposition to LEMAS and other BJS and related research. The literature, including BJS and related federally funded studies, does not address supervisor satisfaction with the transition process, preparedness, and these heretofore seemingly ministerial transitions of power.

Transitions of Power; Formal and Informal Versus Succession Planning

Michelson (2006), as cited by Jarrell and Pewitt (2007), asserts that "many leaders of government agencies lack an exit strategy, offer little evidence of a formal transition, and treat SP [succession planning] as nothing more than lining up personnel for vacancies" (p. 299). Perhaps the most visible example of a formal transition of power occurs every four years in the federal government: the occasion of the election and inauguration of the president of the United States. Whether a one- or two-term president, the framers of the US Constitution realized the need to establish guidelines for the orderly election of (and removal) of the president, vice president, and others in our constitutional system of government. Article II et al. of the US Constitution dictates terms of office (years), qualifications to hold office, and the oath of office (U.S. Const. art. II, § 1–4).

In the present study, respondents were classified into three major public service areas: elected, appointed, or civil service-tested supervisors/commanders. Each of these areas presents its own inherent obstacles to effective transition and succession planning, including tenure limitations and alliances for political officials, often times inflexible civil service rules and regulations, and human resource personnel who may not wish to challenge and/or change the system in place (Green 2000; Schall 1997; as cited by Jarrell and Pewitt 2007). Elkin et al. (2012) further suggest that the presence of a detailed succession plan may additionally reduce undue stress and conflict within the organization. Nowhere within succession planning literature in the public sector, however, is there a codified actual transition process. Since the assassination of President James A. Garfield in 1881 and the passage of the Pendleton Act of 1883, which established a civil service commission and merit-based selection process for the federal service, both formal and informal succession planning processes have been in place ("Pendleton Act," 2014; Pendleton Act of 1883).

In one sense, the US Constitution serves as the most significant succession planning document in the US history. However, nowhere in the US Constitution does specific language appear regarding the actual steps to the formal or informal transition of power, assuming command. Not until the approval of the President

Transition Act of 1963 on March 7, 1964 (and subsequent amendments; Presidential Transitions Effectiveness Act, August 17, 1988; Presidential Transition Act of 2000, October 13, 2000) did the first formal executive transition plan become differentiated from the succession planning heretofore informally established in the US Constitution (President Transition Act of 1963, Public Law § 88–277 [1964]). The purpose of the President Transition Act of 1963 is, in part:

> …to promote the orderly transfer of the executive power in connection with the expiration of the term of office of a President and the inauguration of a new President. The national interest requires that such transitions in the office of President be accomplished so as to assure continuity in the faithful execution of the laws and in the conduct of the affairs of the Federal Government, both domestic and foreign. Any disruption occasioned by the transfer of the executive power could produce results detrimental to the safety and well-being of the United States and its people. Accordingly, it is the intent of the Congress that appropriate actions be authorized and taken to avoid or minimize any disruption. In addition to the specific provisions contained in this Act directed toward that purpose, it is the intent of the Congress that all officers of the Government so conduct the affairs of the Government for which the exercise responsibility and authority as (1) to be mindful of problems occasioned by transitions in the office of President, (2) to take appropriate lawful steps to avoid or minimize disruptions that might be occasioned by the transfer of the executive power, and (3) otherwise to promote orderly transitions in the office of President. (President Transition Act of 1963, Public Law § 88–277, §§ 2, [1964])

The Act goes on to establish such things as authorizing the Administrator of General Services (now the US Office of General Services) to accommodate the president-elect and vice president-elect with the appropriate staff, facilities, and funding to meet the purposes of the Act. The Act concludes by also establishing the orderly transition of the outgoing president and vice president to private life; "for use in connection with winding up the affairs of his office, necessary services and facilities of the same general character as authorized by this act to be provided to Presidents-elect and Vice Presidents-elect" (President Transition Act of 1963, Public Law § 88–277, §§ 4, [1964]). Despite the presence of the US Constitution, and other state constitutions, as well as the President Transition Act of 1963, public agencies and public officers are reluctant to engage in meaningful succession planning (Jarrell and Pewitt 2007, pp. 297–298). We further suggest that formal ministerial acts associated with the actual transition of power in public agencies and among public officers are demonstrably nonexistent within the current literature. Transition planning, both formal and informal, is differentiated from succession planning most notably by the presence of actionable characteristics such as facilities, funding, personnel support, and other related codified requirements and steps (Hogue 2012; Smith 2008; President Transition Act of 1963, Public Law § 88–277, §§ 2–5, [1964]). Succession planning, however, is

> the plan an organization employs to fill its most critical leadership and professional positions (Huang 2001). It is the ongoing, purposeful, and systematic identification of qualified and appropriate successors to leadership, with a commitment to assessing, developing, and investing in organizational leadership to enhance performance, development, and preparedness (Huang 2001; Kim 2003; McDonald 2006, as cited by Jarrell and Pewitt 2007).

McNair (2015) studied eight first-time community college (public) presidents in California and their experiences as they ascended to their new positions. The study was prepared under the premise that 90 % of community college presidents anticipate retiring within 15 years of 2012, thus highlighting the need to heighten the discussion of not only succession planning, but also how potential leaders are groomed for presidencies as well as specifically prepared to transition into their new roles (McNair 2015, p. 72). In 2014, there were 1132 community colleges in the United States (AACC 2014). Unlike community college presidencies, however, thousands of civil service promotions, other appointments, and elections to criminal justice command positions occur daily in the United States and around the world.

In terms of scale, the most recent census of state and local law enforcement agencies conducted by BJS indicates that in the United States, there are 765,000 sworn law enforcement officers across 17,985 state and local law enforcement agencies (U.S. Department of Justice 2011). Assuming arguendo that there is at least one supervisor at each state and local law enforcement agency in the census, we can infer that there are well in excess of 17,000 supervisors that could benefit from not only succession planning, but also a codified transition plan that may yield both a higher level of preparedness and satisfaction once in the command position. The aforementioned literature supports the premise that only on the largest of public sector stages, the election and transition of a president of the United States, do a succession plan (the US Constitution) and codified transition planning efforts occur in a deliberate and relatively methodical manner.

"On November 6, 1980, the President-elect (Ronald W. Reagan) named his formal transition team, a job he described as 'translating campaign promises into reality'" (Smith 2008, p. 16). The focus of succession planning is on who will fill various positions in the absence of others. The focus of transition planning is on the specific process of how a person will assume a new role in a manner that allows them to be more prepared to assume their new position, yielding both a more prepared and more highly satisfied new supervisor. Beyond elected officials who speak of transition teams and transition efforts, the literature is void of this critical process and related discussions for criminal justice and other public administration supervisors and other agency leaders.

Satisfaction and Preparedness

In the current study, the dependent variable of supervisor satisfaction was measured by the question "I am satisfied with the support I received from my agency when I was promoted to my most recent supervisory job" (coded as SUPPORTS). The dependent variable of supervisor preparedness was measured with the question "I feel/felt prepared as a supervisor in my most current job" (coded as PREPAREDP). Six independent variables represented the formal transition process: "I was provided with clear job expectations for my most recent supervisory job prior to starting the assignment" (coded as JOBEXPFT); "There was a written policy/procedure that guided me as I undertook my most recent supervisory job" (coded as WRITGDFT); "There was no orientation provided by my agency as I assumed my most recent supervisory job" (coded as ORIENTFT); "I was required to attend a formal supervisory training outside of my agency as I assumed my most recent supervisory job" (coded as TRAINOUTFT); "I was required to attend a formal supervisory training inside of my agency as I assumed my most recent supervisory job" (coded as TRAININSIDEFT); and "I was supported by a formal transition team and/or mentor as I assumed my most recent supervisory job" (coded as TRANSFORMFT). Three independent variables represented the informal transition process: "There was no support provided to me as I assumed my most recent supervisory job" (coded as NOSUPPORTIT); "I have primarily learned my supervisory skills through observation and my personal experiences" (coded as SKILLSIT); and "I had/have regular meetings with my supervisors as I assume/d my current (most recent, if retired/former) supervisory job" (coded as REGMEETINGSIT). Respondents were offered a six-point scale to measure their response (1 = strongly disagree, 2 = disagree, 3 = slightly disagree, 4 = slightly agree, 5 = agree, and 6 = strongly agree). Additional discussion will appear in later sections.

LEMAS and other BJS and related studies do not assess supervisory preparedness. LEMAS assesses law enforcement agencies in six types of preparedness activities and the corresponding officers dedicated to those activities: emergency preparedness exercises, increased presence at critical areas, dissemination of information to citizens, community meetings, partnering with diverse communities, and public antifear campaigns (U.S. Department of Justice 2011, p. 31). No research could be found that measures the preparedness of individual police supervisors as they assume their new role(s), either in textbooks or in scholarly literature and related sources. This research study may add to the body of the literature that further isolates self-reported perceptions of preparedness and satisfaction in criminal justice supervisors/commanders.

Higgins et al. (2013) studied 136 police middle managers in an attempt to validate M.L. Dantzker's germinal research on police job satisfaction, a similar population to this research study. For the purposes of this study, like Dantzker 1994; Dantzker and Kubin 1998; Locke 1976; and Miller et al. (2009), as cited by Higgins et al. (2013), "job satisfaction refers to a positive appraisal toward one's job" or, in this research study, a positive appraisal toward one's transition/promotional experience(s). According to Herzberg (1973), as cited by Higgins et al. (2013),

> different factors combine to create job satisfaction and dissatisfaction among [an] employee. He identified these as either motivators or hygiene factors. Motivators promote job satisfaction. They include (a) achievement, (b) responsibility, (c) the work itself, (d) recognition, and (e) advancement/promotion. Hygiene factors do not directly lead to job satisfaction among employees. However, their absence may lead to job dissatisfaction. They consist of (a) organizational policies, (b) supervision and leadership, (c) pay or salary, (d) work conditions, and (e) communication with supervisors/work partners. Herzberg contended that employees need to reach an acceptable level of hygiene factors to feel neutral about their jobs. Therefore, employers should seek ways of eliminating dissatisfaction resulting from hygiene factors and focus on improving the motivators in the work environment to increase job satisfaction (pp. 20–21).

Miller et al. (2009) further suggest that "within the discipline of policing, there are relatively few published studies which attempt to identify and explain variables that may contribute to portions of variance in job satisfaction" (p. 419). Miller et al. (2009) further suggest that future research should assess job satisfaction in the context of performance, assuming that a more satisfied police officer will be more effective on the job (p. 425).

Despite differing results in job satisfaction in policing research, primarily due to inconsistent instruments and measurements of job satisfaction as a dependent variable (Higgins et al. 2013), no literature can be found in the United States that measures levels of job satisfaction of police supervisors/commanders with the transition process and level of preparedness as they assumed their supervisory role(s). This research study may add to the literature by further isolating key variables that specifically impact one's satisfaction and preparedness with the transition process, thus yielding a more satisfied supervisor who performs more effectively in their new supervisory roles (Miller et al. 2009).

Methodology

The purpose of this quantitative cross-sectional survey research was to examine whether or not the presence or absence of a formal or informal transition process resulted in higher levels of employee job satisfaction and preparedness (dependent variables) of members at two New York State criminal justice associations and their self-reported perceptions of job satisfaction and preparedness after promotion or appointment into a command role. The research methodology was quantitative, using a cross-sectional survey design to collect and analyze "data at one point in time" (Brown 2007; Creswell 2005, p. 355), primarily because of time limitations and the financial commitment that a longitudinal study would involve. Qualitative data were also collected in the form of open-ended questions to capture expanded responses of survey participants (Appendix D).

Demographics

Participants in this research included sworn (current or retired) criminal justice supervisors/commanders of two New York State criminal justice agency associations. The potential pool of survey participants or the target population was approximately 1237 members between the two associations (N = 1237). It is believed that each association, with its respective membership characteristics, is representative of the universe of criminal justice command (supervisory)-level personnel in the United States. The two associations chosen for the study are not specifically referred to in order to ensure participant confidentiality. Both associations are located in New York State, and both have tightly restricted primary

Table 1 Participant characteristics—employee title (n = 200)

Category / Strata	Population (N = 1237)	Response (raw)	Response percentage	Response percentage versus population
Commissioner/Super. (retired)		2	1	0.162
Chief of Police (retired)		13	6.5	1.05
Lieutenant (retired)		1	0.5	0.080
Sergeant (retired)		1	0.5	0.080
Other supervisor (retired)		1	0.5	0.080
Commissioner/Super. (active)		9	4.5	0.728
Chief of Police (active)		49	24.5	3.96
Sheriff (active)		22	11.0	1.78
Asst./ Dep. Chief/Super. (active)		6	3	0.485
Undersheriff (active)		13	6.5	1.05
Commander/Major (active)		7	3.5	0.566
Chief Deputy (active)		7	3.5	0.566
Captain (active)		16	8	1.29
Lieutenant (active)		15	7.5	1.21
Sergeant (active)		24	12	1.94
Other supervisor (active)		14	7	1.13
Total		200	100	16.16

membership to supervisory/command-level personnel only. These associations were selected because of their relative similarities in organizational structure and because both associations' organizational leadership gave permission for the administration of a survey to their respective membership.

Of the 1237 members of the population selected for this study, 205, or 16.6 %, responded to the survey. Following national trend lines in this area of criminal justice research, 92 % of respondents to the gender question (185) for this research study were males, while 8 % of respondents (17) were female (Johnson 2012, p. 162). Ninety-eight percent of respondents self-reported as being white, one percent self-reported as black, African American, or Negro, and 1 % self-reported as Hispanic, Latino, or of Spanish origin. In addition, 35.5 % of the respondents to the employee title question (71) were active chiefs of police or sheriffs (Table 1) with an age range of 31–75 across all survey respondents. Twenty-nine percent of respondents (59) self-reported that they had completed a bachelor's degree, while

Table 2 Participant characteristics—Education Level Completed (n = 201)

	Response percentage	Response count
General education degree (GED)	0.5	1
High school diploma	6.0	12
Some college credits (no degree earned)	23.9	48
Associate's degree	22.4	45
Bachelor's degree	29.4	59
Master's degree	16.4	33
Doctoral degree	1.5	3
		201

16 % (33) self-reported that they had completed their master's degree and three respondents had completed their doctoral degree (Table 2).

Population

According to Creswell (2005), a sample "is a subgroup of the target population that the researcher plans to study for the purpose of making generalization about the target population" (p. 398). The sample is a small group that, if studied correctly, produces findings that can be generalized to the entire population. To survey all criminal justice supervisors/commanders in the United States is neither possible nor necessary. The goal of the research was to obtain data from a small, manageable, and representative group (Brown 2007; Creswell 2005).

Creswell (2005) further stated that "to reduce sampling error, select as large a sample from the population as possible. The larger the sample, the more the participants will be representative of the entire population" (p. 359). It was not expected that the results of the research would be fully generalizable to the overall criminal justice supervisor/commander population within the United States, and this was acknowledged as a limitation of the research study.

Neuman (2003) stated that "a researcher samples so he or she can draw inferences from the sample to the population. Researchers are not interested in samples in themselves; they want to infer to the population" (p. 233). Neuman further noted, "Everything else being equal, the larger the sample size, the smaller the sampling error" (p. 233).

While sampling error is a part of all research, efforts to maximize the generalizability of the study's findings to the entire population of criminal justice agency supervisors/commanders were maximized by "hav[ing] a good sampling frame list, as large a sample from the population as possible [in light of survey constraints], use of a good instrument, and rigorous administration procedures" (Brown 2007; Creswell 2005, p. 360). The use of sound quantitative research methods enhanced the veracity of the results and credibility of the final conclusions and recommendations of the research. The literature suggested that sampling an entire population is not advisable, cost-effective, or efficient, but it can provide a sound basis for further research (Neuman 2003; Su 2006). Su (2006), as cited by Brown (2007), studied 632 accounting students in the United States and Taiwan and concluded that the small sample selected might not be generalizable to the population of US or Taiwanese accounting students and that the characteristics of the students might not be similar to the overall population. However, generalizability need not be the only measure of successful research. Su further concluded,

> The findings of the present study are essential to training the new generation in learning how to avoid the pitfalls of inappropriate decision making that have underlying cultural differences and promote clear decision for effective implementation. This study can begin to help international managers better understand how business ethics is perceived and conducted across cultures. This research is laying the foundation for further research in cross-cultural ethics in accounting. (pp. 156–157)

Lee et al. (2006) studied over 8400 kindergarten students across the United States in 50 school districts. Lee et al. noted that small samples, short-term research, and studies "lacking in scientific rigor" were contributing factors to poor historical research (p. 170). Lee et al. secured substantial funding from the US Department of Education to conduct a costly longitudinal study of kindergarten students. While the present research was neither longitudinal nor financially supported, it exhibited strong scientific rigor. While the sample population was not generalizable to the entire criminal justice supervisor/command population in the United States, it nonetheless exhibited strong characteristics of that larger population (Lee et al. 2006; Su 2006).

According to Gay (1996), "at approximately $N = 5000$ and beyond, the population size is almost irrelevant and a sample size of 400 is adequate. Thus, the larger the population, the smaller the percentage needed to get a representative sample" (p. 125). The use of sound quantitative methods enhanced the veracity of the results and the credibility of the conclusions and recommendations only insofar as the population of both associations was concerned (Brown 2007). While the final sample studied in this research could not be scientifically generalized to the entire population of criminal justice supervisors/commanders in the United States, some commonalities could be identified that can provide criminal justice and other public administration agency leaders with a template for current action within their organizations and guidelines for future research (Brown 2007).

The target population of two New York State criminal justice associations ($N = 1237$) is small in comparison with the overall US population of sworn police officers since it represents only 0.027 % of 765,000. The characteristics of the target population selected for the present study closely represented the greater population. The population of the two associations selected, however, exhibited characteristics that have been established by the US Department of Justice as those common to sworn law enforcement officers and police supervisors/commanders (U.S. Department of Justice 2011).

Sampling

The data were collected through the use of the electronic survey tool SurveyMonkey®, and analysis was completed utilizing both Microsoft Excel® and SPSS® version 22. A prepared letter from the principal and coinvestigators, in the form of an e-mail with an embedded link (Appendix A), was forwarded by association e-mail administrators to all association members. Two follow-up/reminder e-mails were sent to maximize response rates. Informed consent, voluntariness, confidentiality, and institutional review board (IRB) approval and related discussions were also contained in the survey cover letter. Survey data were exported from the online tool into Microsoft Excel®. A codebook was constructed, and the Microsoft Excel® worksheet was formatted with the proper codes and then imported into SPSS® version 22 for final statistical analysis. Although the sample for the overall research study was $n = 205$, some of the surveys returned were incomplete. In the case of missing data, SPSS® created a *listwise exclusion* and discarded the entire case for consideration of the particular analysis where data needed for the calculation were omitted. Next, we will discuss our analysis process and our research findings.

Findings and Discussion

Prior sections discussed the selection, planning, administration, and evaluation of the survey instrument as the basis for the collection of the primary data for the research. The research design and its appropriateness were discussed, and data collection and analysis procedures were described, along with some findings. This section presents the detailed results and statistical findings as well as further discussion. Finally, the results and findings are presented in the context of each of the research questions and hypotheses, leading to the conclusions and recommendations found in the final section of this article.

The purpose of this quantitative cross-sectional survey research was to examine whether or not the presence or absence of a formal or informal transition process resulted in higher levels of employee job satisfaction and preparedness (dependent variables) of members at two New York State criminal justice associations and their self-reported perceptions of job satisfaction and preparedness after promotion or appointment into a command role.

Variable Analysis

As we have discussed, in the current study, the dependent variable of supervisor satisfaction was measured by the question “I am satisfied with the support I received from my agency when I was promoted to my most recent supervisory job" (coded as SUPPORTS). The dependent variable of supervisor preparedness was measured with the question "I feel/felt prepared as a supervisor in my most current job" (coded as PREPAREDP). Six independent variables represented the formal transition process: "I was provided with clear job expectations for my most recent supervisory job prior to starting the assignment" (coded as JOBEXPFT); "There was a written policy/procedure that guided me as I undertook my most recent supervisory job" (coded as WRITGDFT); "There was no orientation provided by my agency as I assumed my most recent supervisory job" (coded as ORIENTFT); "I was required to attend a formal supervisory training outside of my agency as I assumed my most recent supervisory job" (coded as TRAINOUTFT); "I was required to attend a formal supervisory training inside of my agency as I assumed my most recent supervisory job" (coded as TRAININSIDEFT); and "I was supported by a formal transition team and/or mentor as I assumed my most recent supervisory job" (coded as TRANSFORMFT).

Three independent variables represented the informal transition process: "There was no support provided to me as I assumed my most recent supervisory job" (coded as NOSUPPORTIT); "I have primarily learned my supervisory skills through observation and my personal experiences" (coded as SKILLSIT); and "I had/have regular meetings with my supervisors as I assume/d my current (most recent, if retired/former) supervisory job" (coded as REGMEETINGSIT). Respondents were offered a six-point scale to measure their response (1 = strongly disagree, 2 = disagree, 3 = slightly disagree, 4 = slightly agree, 5 = agree, and 6 = strongly agree). The authors selected these variables based on their collective experiences in various command-level criminal justice leadership roles as they related to both formal and informal transition activities.

Of the six (6) independent variables that represent the formal transition (FT) process, as generated against all cases, four (4) were statistically significant as they impacted self-reported levels of preparedness (JOBEXP-FT, WRITGD-FT, ORIENT-FT and TRAININSIDE-FT) and five (5) were statistically significant as they impacted self-reported levels of satisfaction (JOBEXP-FT, WRITGD-FT, ORIENT-FT, TRAININSIDE-FT, and TRANSFORM-FT). Of the three (3) independent variables that represent the informal transition process (IT), as generated against all cases, two (2) were statistically significant as they impacted self-reported levels of preparedness (NOSUPPORT-IT and REGMEETINGS-IT), and all three (3) were statistically significant as they impacted self-reported levels of satisfaction (NOSUPPORT-IT, SKILLS-IT, and REGMEETINGS-IT [Table 6]).

In the command-only cases, however, only one (1) of six (6) formal transition (FT) independent variables were both statistically significant and highly correlated as they impacted self-reported levels of preparedness (JOBEXP-FT [Table 6]). Likewise, only one (1) independent variable that represented the informal transition (IT) process was statistically significant as it impacted self-reported levels of preparedness (REGMEETINGS-IT). Likewise, two (2) of six (6) independent variables representing the formal transition (FT) process were statistically significant as they impacted self-reported levels of satisfaction (JOBEXP-FT, WRITGD-FT).

Two (2) of three (3) independent variables represented the informal transition (IT) process were statistically significant as they impacted self-reported levels of satisfaction (NOSUPPORT-IT, SKILLS-IT [Table 6]).

Table 3 represents the frequency distribution(s) of the independent and dependent variables noted herein (Table 3). Detailed frequency distribution histograms for each variable are contained in Appendix C. Table 4 represents Pearson's correlation coefficient (PCC) for each of the 11 independent and dependent variables against all cases (listwise exclusion where n = 205). Table 5 represents PCC for each of the 11 independent and dependent variables against all active/retired agency head employee titles (EMPTITLE = Commissioner/Superintendent, Chief of Police, or Sheriff), listwise exclusion where n = 95. Table 6 represents a simple linear regression analysis of the total population who responded to the survey (n = 205), as compared to an isolated subset of the total survey respondents that the authors determined were significant enough to compare. Of the 205 overall respondents to the survey, 95 represented senior command-level staff. These were represented in the survey and coded as EMPTITLE (employee title [Table 1]). These titles represented active and retired criminal justice commissioners and superintendents, as well as chiefs of police and sheriffs, and represented 46 % of the overall respondents to the survey.

Recommendations and Conclusion

The results of this study show that for the overall sample population (n = 205), a statistically significant correlation exists between having clear job expectations when entering a new supervisory position and the new supervisor's high levels of self-reported satisfaction and preparedness as they transitioned into their new command position. This study represents the first known analysis in the United States that yields a comprehensive, actionable, criminal justice Command Transition Matrix© tool.

Limitations and Future Research

As the study developed, it was acknowledged that the study would be subject to the following limitations:

1. Only individuals who agreed to participate voluntarily would be surveyed.
2. A limited population and the limited time available to conduct the research might have reduced the data set.
3. Convenience sampling does not provide the same power of generalizability as random sampling, but the target population was known to exhibit similar

Table 3 Frequency distribution percentages—all independent and dependent variables, all cases

		JOBEXP-FT	WRITGD-FT	ORIENT-FT	TRAINOUT-FT	TRAININSIDE-FT	TRANSFORM-FT	NOSUPPORT-IT	SKILLS-IT	REGMEETINGS-IT	SUPPORT-S	PREPARED-P
N	Valid *n*=	190	190	188	186	188	190	189	189	187	190	189
	Missing	15	15	17	19	17	15	16	16	18	15	16
Coding	Selection	% *n*	% *n*	% *n*	% *n*	% *n*	% *n*	% *n*	% *n*	% *n*	% *n*	% *n*
1	Strongly disagree	3.7	11.1	6.9	21.0	23.9	20.5	16.9	0.5	3.7	1.6	1.6
2	Disagree	11.6	23.7	14.9	38.7	46.3	43.2	32.8	2.6	10.7	6.8	3.7
3	Slightly disagree	6.3	13.7	11.7	8.6	11.2	8.9	17.5	2.6	9.1	5.3	4.8
4	Slightly agree	22.1	22.1	14.9	4.8	5.9	8.4	18.5	10.6	18.2	17.4	16.9
5	Agree	37.4	22.1	30.3	16.7	8.5	13.7	7.9	45.0	37.4	41.1	47.6
6	Strongly agree	18.9	7.4	21.3	10.2	4.3	5.3	6.3	38.6	20.9	27.9	25.4
	Total	100.0	100.0	100.0	100.0	100.0	100.0	100.0	100.0	100.0	100.0	100.0

Table 4 Pearson's correlation coefficient (PCC) for 11 independent and dependent variables against all cases

		JOBEXP-FT	WRITGD-FT	ORIENT-FT	TRAINOUT-FT	TRAININSIDE-FT	TRANSFORM-FT	NOSUPPORT-IT	SKILLS-IT	REGMEETINGS-IT	SUPPORT-S	PREPARED-P
JOBEXP-FT	PCC	1	0.294**	−0.314**	0.222**	0.312**	0.260**	−0.306**	−0.189*	0.187*	0.468**	0.442**
	Sig. (2-tailed)		0.000	0.000	0.003	0.000	0.001	0.000	0.013	0.014	0.000	0.000
WRITGD−FT	PCC	0.294**	1	−0.264**	0.322**	0.390**	0.317**	−0.180*	−0.147	0.026	0.216**	0.144
	Sig. (2-tailed)	0.000		0.000	0.000	0.000	0.000	0.018	0.055	0.739	0.004	0.06
ORIENT-FT	PCC	−0.314**	−0.264**	1	−0.321**	−0.436**	−0.434**	0.546**	0.156*	−0.210**	−0.250**	−0.150*
	Sig. (2-tailed)	0.000	0.000		0.000	0.000	0.000	0.000	0.04	0.006	0.001	0.049
TRAINOUT-FT	PCC	0.222**	0.322**	−0.321**	1	0.618**	0.199**	−0.178*	−0.194*	0.051	0.084	0.069
	Sig. (2-tailed)	0.003	0.000	0.000		0.000	0.009	0.019	0.011	0.505	0.275	0.369
TRAININSIDE-FT	PCC	0.312**	0.390**	−0.436**	0.618**	1	0.379**	−0.252**	−0.225**	0.190*	0.172*	0.169*
	Sig. (2-tailed)	0.000	0.000	0.000	0.000		0.000	0.001	0.003	0.012	0.024	0.027
TRANSFORM-FT	PCC	0.260**	0.317**	−0.434**	0.199**	0.379**	1	−0.267**	−0.091	0.244**	0.238**	0.145
	Sig. (2-tailed)	0.001	0.0000	0	0.009	0.000		0.000	0.234	0.001	0.002	0.057
NOSUPPORT-IT	PCC	−0.306**	−0.180*	0.546**	−0.178*	−0.252**	−0.267**	1	0.212**	−0.213**	−0.352**	−0.147
	Sig. (2-tailed)	0.000	0.018	0.000	0.019	0.001	0.000		0.005	0.005	0.000	0.054
SKILLS-IT	PCC	−0.189*	−0.147	0.156*	−0.194*	−0.225**	−0.091	0.212**	1	−0.067	−0.192*	−0.054
	Sig. (2-tailed)	0.013	0.055	0.040	0.011	0.003	0.234	0.005		0.381	0.011	0.483
REGMEETINGS-IT	PCC	0.187*	0.026	−0.210**	0.051	0.190*	0.244**	−0.213**	−0.067	1	0.209**	0.294**
	Sig. (2-tailed)	0.014	0.739	0.006	0.505	0.012	0.001	0.005	0.381		0.006	0
SUPPORT-S	PCC	0.468**	0.216**	−0.250**	0.084	0.172*	0.238**	−0.352**	−0.192*	0.209**	1	0.263**
	Sig. (2-tailed)	0.000	0.004	0.001	0.275	0.024	0.002	0.000	0.011	0.006		0.000
PREPARED-P	PCC	0.442**	0.144	−0.150*	0.069	0.169*	0.145	−0.147	−0.054	0.294**	0.263**	1
	Sig. (2-tailed)	0.000	0.06	0.049	0.369	0.027	0.057	0.054	0.483	0.000	0.000	

*Correlation is significant at the 0.05 level (2-tailed)

**Correlation is significant at the 0.01 level (2-tailed)

c. Listwise $N = 172$

Table 5 Pearson's correlation coefficient (PCC) for each of the 11 independent and dependent variables against all active/retired agency head employee titles

		JOBEXP-FT	WRITGD-FT	ORIENT-FT	TRAINOUT-FT	TRAININSIDEFT	TRANSFORM-FT	NOSUPPORT-IT	SKILLS-IT	REGMEETINGS-IT	SUPPORT-S	PREPARED-P
JOBEXP-FT	PCC	1	0.253*	−0.235*	0.323**	0.286**	0.196	−0.199	−0.174	0.087	0.335**	0.231*
	Sig. (2-tailed)		0.023	0.035	0.003	0.01	0.079	0.076	0.121	0.44	0.002	0.038
WRITGD-FT	PCC	0.253*	1	−0.284*	0.301**	0.331**	0.217	−0.024	−0.132	0.032	0.268*	−0.004
	Sig. (2-tailed)	0.023		0.010	0.006	0.003	0.051	0.833	0.239	0.777	0.016	0.971
ORIENT-FT	PCC	−0.235*	−0.284*	1	−0.314**	−0.314**	−0.353**	0.524**	0.237*	−0.051	−0.067	−0.055
	Sig. (2-tailed)	0.035	0.010		0.004	0.004	0.001	0	0.033	0.648	0.555	0.623
TRAINOUT-FT	PCC	0.323**	0.301**	−0.314**	1	0.603**	0.104	−0.131	−0.285**	−0.026	0.219*	0.073
	Sig. (2-tailed)	0.003	0.006	0.004		0	0.355	0.245	0.010	0.817	0.05	0.516
TRAININSIDE-FT	PCC	0.286**	0.331**	−0.314**	0.603**	1	0.213	−0.106	−0.119	0.129	0.023	0.059
	Sig. (2-tailed)	0.01	0.003	0.004	0		0.057	0.345	0.292	0.25	0.842	0.601
TRANSFORM-FT	PCC	0.196	0.217	−0.353**	0.104	0.213	1	−0.078	−0.088	0.074	0.095	0.149
	Sig. (2-tailed)	0.079	0.051	0.001	0.355	0.057		0.487	0.436	0.509	0.401	0.186
NOSUPPORT-IT	PCC	−0.199	−0.024	0.524**	−0.131	−0.106	−0.078	1	0.286**	−0.063	−0.265*	0.017
	Sig. (2-tailed)	0.076	0.833	0	0.245	0.345	0.487		0.010	0.576	0.017	0.879
SKILLS-IT	PCC	−0.174	−0.132	0.237*	−0.285**	−0.119	−0.088	0.286**	1	0.038	−0.196	0.051
	Sig. (2-tailed)	0.121	0.239	0.033	0.010	0.292	0.436	0.010		0.736	0.08	0.652
REGMEETINGS-IT	*PCC*	*0.087*	*0.032*	*−0.051*	*−0.026*	*0.129*	*0.074*	*−0.063*	*0.038*	*1*	*−0.013*	*0.138*
	Sig. (2-tailed)	0.440	0.777	0.648	0.817	0.25	0.509	0.576	0.736		0.91	0.22
SUPPORT-S	PCC	0.335**	0.268*	−0.067	0.219*	0.023	0.095	−0.265*	−0.196	−0.013	1	0.007
	Sig. (2-tailed)	0.002	0.016	0.555	0.050	0.842	0.401	0.017	0.08	0.91		0.95
PREPARED-P	PCC	0.231*	−0.004	−0.055	0.073	0.059	0.149	0.017	0.051	0.138	0.007	1
	Sig. (2-tailed)	0.038	0.971	0.623	0.516	0.601	0.186	0.879	0.652	0.22	0.95	

EMPTITLE = Commissioner/Superintendent, Chief of Police, or Sheriff

*Correlation is significant at the 0.05 level (2-tailed)

**Correlation is significant at the 0.01 level (2-tailed)

c. Listwise $N = 81$

Table 6 Simple linear regression analysis—all cases versus command cases

Independent variable	Dependent variable	All cases (n = 205)**		Command cases (n = 95)**	
	Preparedness = PREPARED-P	r	p	r	p
JOBEXP-FT		0.173	0.000*	0.083	0.006*
WRITGD-FT		0.029	0.019*	0.016	0.237ns
ORIENT-FT		0.033	0.014*	0.015	0.245ns
TRAINOUT-FT		0.009	0.206ns	0.003	0.601ns
TRAININSIDE-FT		0.032	0.014*	0.008	0.410ns
TRANSFORM-FT		0.016	0.082ns	0.032	0.095ns
NOSUPPORT-IT		0.026	0.028*	0.007	0.437ns
SKILLS-IT		0.001	0.642ns	0	0.911ns
REGMEETINGS-IT		0.095	0.000*	0.047	0.044*
	Satisfaction = SUPPORTS-S	r	p	r	p
JOBEXP-FT		0.247	0.000*	0.134	0.000*
WRITGD-FT		0.064	0.000*	0.092	0.004*
ORIENT-FT		0.049	0.002*	0.01	0.355ns
TRAINOUT-FT		0.008	0.225ns	0.040	0.065ns
TRAININSIDE-FT		0.038	0.008*	0.0010	0.783ns
TRANSFORM-FT		0.064	0.000*	0.015	0.261ns
NOSUPPORT-IT		0.102	0.000*	0.076	0.009*
SKILLS-IT		0.044	0.004*	0.043	0.052*
REGMEETINGS-IT		0.044	0.004*	0.004	0.539ns

ns $p > 0.05$
*$p < 0.05$
**Listwise exclusion
FT = formal transition
IT = informal transition

characteristics to other populations of criminal justice supervisors within the United States (Gay and Airasian 2000).

4. Data were collected from participants by means of self-reporting of responses, a procedure known to produce bias.
5. Some of the participants might have known the researchers and might have positive or negative feelings that might have affected their responses.
6. The quantitative cross-sectional research design might have had the inherent limitation that the participants' mind-set at the specific time the survey was completed might have caused outlier-type responses related to the respondents' emotional disposition during survey completion.

No research could be found that measures the preparedness of individual police supervisors as they assume their new role(s), either in textbooks or in scholarly literature and related sources. This research study may add to the body of the literature that further isolates self-reported perceptions of preparedness and satisfaction in criminal justice supervisors/commanders. Future research should be conducted utilizing a larger population, perhaps embedded in other standardized agency surveys currently in place, thus limiting oversurveying of the general population and individual survey fatigue.

As we have noted, despite differing results in job satisfaction in policing research, primarily due to inconsistent instruments and measurements of job satisfaction as a dependent variable (Higgins et al. 2013), no literature can be found in the United States that measures levels of job satisfaction of police supervisors/commanders with the transition process and level of preparedness as they assumed their supervisory role(s). Future researchers should strive to build on the present study by developing a standardized measurement tool for both satisfaction and preparedness, similar to the efforts of M.L. Dantzker's (and others) germinal research on police job satisfaction, a similar population to this research study (Dantzker 1994; Dantzker and Kubin 1998; Locke 1976; Miller et al. (2009), as cited by Higgins et al. (2013).

Taken in tandem, the quantitative data provided herein, along with a content analysis of the qualitative data provided in Appendix D and the collective experiences of the authors, yield a comprehensive, actionable, criminal justice Command Transition Matrix© tool (Fig. 1). The genesis of this Command Transition Matrix© tool was the formation of a formal transition team in 2010 for the then Oneida County, New York Sheriff-elect Robert M. Maciol. Perhaps the most meaningful deliverable to come out of the combination of this quantitative and qualitative analysis is the Command Transition Matrix© tool that will serve to guide future criminal justice and other senior public administration elected, appointed, and civil service leaders with the requisite toolbox to both prepare future leaders within their organizations and guide them through the heretofore seemingly ministerial but mission-critical transition between supervisory roles.

The Maciol Transition Team—A Brief History

Robert M. Maciol was elected to the position of Oneida County Sheriff in November 2010. Oneida County, located in upstate New York, has a population of approximately 243,000 with its sheriff's office consisting of 500 employees and a budget of $28 million (2010). While Sheriff-elect Maciol did have limited public administration experience, serving several terms as a part-time mayor in a small village, he did have law enforcement experience serving as a patrolman in a village other than the one he served as mayor. Maciol's law enforcement experience was limited to patrol operations and did not include any management functions such as budgeting, personnel administration, accreditation, and labor relations. Essentially, Maciol was elected to a position for which he had limited or no experience or training.

In New York State, County Sheriffs are Constitutional Officers and are elected with a four-year term. There are no prerequisite requirements for this position other than the person running for the position of sheriff must not have been convicted of a

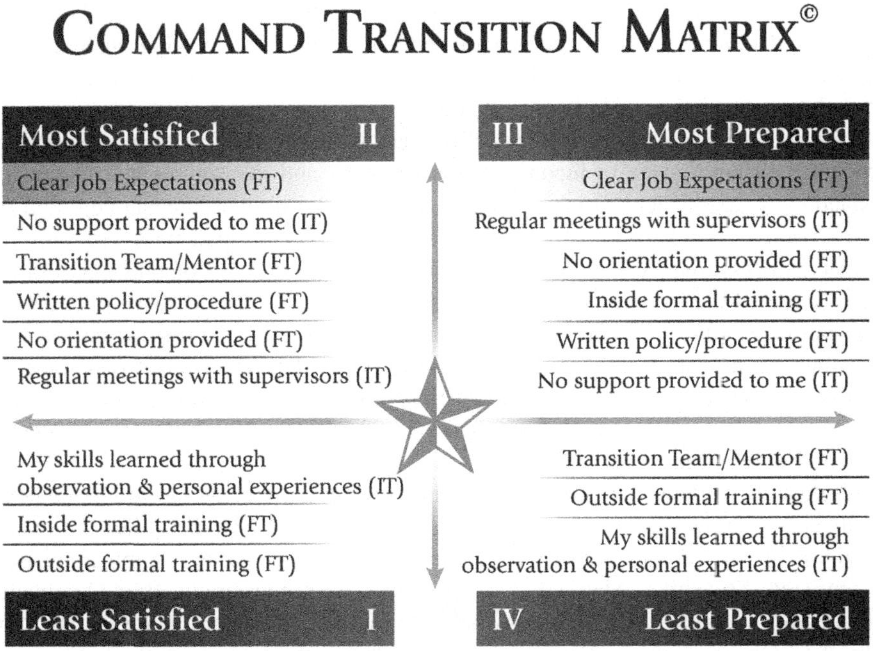

Fig. 1 Command Transition Matrix©—an actionable tool developed based up this research that yields a more satisfied and more prepared supervisor who engages in activities found in quadrant II and quadrant III

felony. As an elected Constitutional Officer, a sheriff answers directly to the electorate of the county in which he or she serves. While the sheriff does not answer to a county manager or supervisor, the position is responsible to the elected county legislators for the agency's operating budget. A sheriff's department in New York State has three operating divisions: Law Enforcement, Civil, and Corrections. The Corrections division is usually the largest of the three in terms of budget and personnel. "Police" departments in New York State do not have a "corrections" function other than perhaps having a limited holding area for prisoners. After an arrestee is arraigned before a judge, it is the County Sheriff's responsibility under the law to maintain that prisoner throughout the legal process. Having a corrections responsibility requires experienced and dedicated staff, especially in a command position.

Raymond L. Philo, a professor of practice in criminal justice at Utica College, former chief of police in New Hartford, New York, and one of the authors of this research project, was asked by Sheriff-elect Maciol to serve on his campaign committee in the spring of 2010. As Maciol was running as a democrat in a predominately republican county, the odds were against this candidate. As such, during the campaign little thought was given to transition should Maciol win the election. Maciol did in fact win the Oneida County Sheriff's election by a substantive majority.

Professor Philo received a phone call two days after the election victory from the Maciol campaign manager, Jordan MacNamara. MacNamara inquired if Philo would be interested in applying for a senior management position in Maciol's administration. Philo indicated he was not interested in leaving his position with Utica College and was subsequently asked whether he would be available to assist the sheriff-elect in assembling a group of law enforcement and corrections professionals who would help Maciol transition to the Sheriff's post. Philo agreed to continue to assist Sheriff-elect Maciol and also suggested another individual with law enforcement and public administrative experience, Dr. James C. Brown, another coauthor of this study, then serving as a vice president at Utica College (now a full-time faculty member in criminal justice). Because Brown had served as the chief deputy at the Oneida County Sheriff's office years earlier, responsible for the department's law enforcement and civil division operations, Philo suggested to MacNamara and Maciol that Brown serves as chairman of a formal transition team. Sheriff-elect Maciol agreed to the establishment of a formal transition committee with Brown and Philo as two of the three members. The Sheriff-elect, along with Philo and Brown, recognized that the third member of the transition committee should be a recognized expert in county-level corrections administration. Chief Anthony Callisto, Jr., another coauthor of this study, quickly emerged as a local, state, and national expert in the correction field, having served as the former chief deputy of the Onondaga County, New York Sheriff's office, and who at the time (2010) was serving as chief of the department of public safety at Syracuse University. Chief Callisto, also an author on this paper, now serves as the senior vice president for the division of campus safety and emergency services at Syracuse University. The collective experience of the Maciol transition team yielded both the need for this study and the following core elements described herein.

The Transition Team—The Transition Command Matrix

Assuming command of a larger organization may require a team effort. A transition team can provide guidance and support to an incoming commander in several ways. While a team may include current members of the new commander's organization, a group of experienced colleagues who are not part of the organization can offer an unbiased and non-conflicted perspective and support the development of goals and objectives that focus more on service to and needs of the community than on the specific desires of personnel within the organization. Ideally, transition team members will have varied experiences, have led organizations themselves, have topical knowledge of the role of the criminal justice or other public administration organization, and have excellent leadership and collaboration skills. The following are some command transition actions that a transition team can perform to assist a new commanding officer.

Building the operational command team. A review of the current organizational chart, written directives related to organization and authority, and any documentation associated with goals or strategic plans can be very helpful in determining where the organization has been and the direction in which the former administration intended it to move. A transition team can review this information and assist the new commander in beginning to formulate priorities in goals, update the vision and mission, and develop a short-term and/or midterm strategic plan (six months to one year). Further, in executive-level command transitions, the team can assist in the review of top-level position descriptions, offer recommendations for appropriate amendments, and assist the new commander with the selection process for a new operational command team.

Budget review and financial and other audits. New commanding officers will need to study and understand the budget for their unit, division, or department. Certainly, a budget prepared by a prior administration will not necessarily be aligned with the goals of the new commander. The transition team should work closely with the new commander on a budget review (including current budget and three previous years for historical perspective), assist in the development of immediate and realistic goals, determine whether any changes can be made to the existing budget, and begin to formulate a strategy for the next budget cycle, focused on the mission, vision, and goals developed in a review and visioning process. The team should also review the most recent end-of-year budget reports to determine how much was actually expended and if there is an "rollover" of funds available from the previous year.

The transition team can also assist in the development of a strategy for auditing the financial records of the prior administration to ensure the new administration can begin with balanced accounts and address any red flags raised during such audit. Confidential funds should be accounted for, and policies for use of such funds should be reviewed. Any bank accounts should be reviewed, and signature changeovers to the new administration should be prepared. Additionally, a complete review of equipment policies, especially "take home vehicle" policies, should be conducted by the transition team, with an eye toward ensuring that the direct assignment of any vehicles is absolutely necessary and appropriate. It is also important for the team to develop a strategy for the review and audit of property and evidence procedures, processing, security, and return/destruction. Critical areas of this review should include detailed inventories with a special focus on weapons, cash, valuable items, and drugs.

Annual report review. The transition team should review the prior three-year annual reports to uncover and trends, highlights, and concerns. The review should also determine whether the organization has been accomplishing goals and objectives and whether there has been any accountability for unrealized goals. This can be helpful as the team assists the new commander in the development of a strategic plan. Further, any other periodic reports prepared by each unit within the new command should be reviewed.

Labor contracts. For organizations with collective bargaining units, the transition team should review the current labor agreements, contracts, and memoranda of understanding to ensure that the development of a strategic plan and the amendment of any policies, procedures, or processes do not violate such agreements. The team should meet with labor leaders to understand their unique issues and concerns and assist the new commander in the development of a joint labor/management strategy.

Engaging the former administration. The transition team should interview the former commander and command team to understand current challenges and issues that will confront the new administration. The discussion should focus on the experiences, insights, problems faced, and most recent concerns. This information, along with the information gathered from labor leaders, can be taken in context as the transition team assists in the development of a strategic plan. In a negatively charged political atmosphere, this may be extremely difficult or even impossible to accomplish. Subordinate staff to the current administration may not feel comfortable talking to the incoming administration in this type of an environment. The transition team must be sensitive to this reality and be able to navigate these difficult waters.

Visiting and inspecting facilities. The transition team should visit all facilities that will be under the command of the new administration and positively interact with staff assigned to such facilities. The team should field questions about the new commander, ask questions about the use and condition of the facilities, and learn about the top issues of concern that officers and staff have. Such concerns can be considered during the development of a strategic plan. A friendly approach by the commander and team members can ease natural concerns related to the command transition and offer opportunities for relationship building.

Commanding officer's introduction to department staff. Effective transitions include a period of listening. New commanding officers, who visit all ranks of staff, listen to their stories, their highlights, and their concerns, and take opportunities to resolve "low-hanging fruit" issues confronting staff, will create opportunities to establish rapport and credibility. Direction and delegation should be given relatively slowly, at a pace that respects the work of those who have been in command and the current staff being introduced to a new commander and a new command style. At the same time, top-level decisions regarding tactical issues, purchasing of important and needed equipment, and administrative structure can quickly establish the leadership of the new commander and offer a view of the value that this commander and the command team will bring to the organization. Of course it will be very important for the new commander and command team to effectively communicate changes prior to implementation and clearly articulate and communicate rationale for changes made.

Commanding officer's introduction to the community served. While meeting and listening to staff is important, meeting and listening to constituents in the community is equally important. A well-balanced transition team can provide support to the commander with making community connections, offering introductions to various community leaders, community groups, and individuals. The new commander should be able to articulate a clear sense of vision and be fully prepared to listen to the ideas, concerns, and suggestions from community members. These ideas can be used to refine and fully develop a strategic plan for the organization and offer a new commanding officer an opportunity to build bridges in the community.

Conclusion

Screening for levels of satisfaction and preparedness after promotion or appointment into a command role is not prevalent in the United States but is needed to provide leaders with an inventory of potential predictive characteristics which may improve these transitions of power (Brown 2007). The current research study provides criminal justice and other public administration leaders with new insights with respect to recognizing the formal and informal transition factors that affect their employees and using this understanding to implement preventive, mitigating, and corrective measures toward the implementation of an effective codified Command Transition Matrix© tool, thus yielding a more satisfied and more well-prepared supervisor.

The results of this study show that for the overall sample population (n = 205), a statistically significant correlation exists between having clear job expectations when entering a new supervisory position and the new supervisor's high levels of self-reported satisfaction and preparedness as they transitioned into their new command position. Qualitative data contained herein further emphasize the overall lack of limited to no formal codified transition process as new criminal justice and other public administration elected, appointed, and civil service leaders assume their new roles.

References

American Association of Community Colleges (AACC). (2014). 2014 fact sheet. Retrieved from http://www.aacc.nche.edu/AboutCC/Documents/Facts14_Data_R3.pdf

Brown, J. C. (2007). Full- and part-time employee stress and job satisfaction at two upstate New York colleges. *Dissertation Abstracts International, 68*(08) (UMI No. 3277201).

Creswell, J. W. (2005). *Educational research: Planning, conducting, and evaluating quantitative and qualitative research*. Upper Saddle River, NJ: Pearson.

Dantzker, M. L., & Kubin, B. (1998). Job satisfaction: The gender perspective among police officers. *American Journal of Criminal Justice, 23*(1), 19–31. Retrieved from http://www.springer.com/social+sciences/criminology/journal/12103

Dube, L., & Pare, G. (2003). Rigor in information systems positivist case research: Current practices, trends and recommendations. *MIS Quarterly, 27*(4), 597–635. Retrieved from EBSCOhost database, July 22, 2006.

Elkin, G., Smith, K., & Zhang, H. (2012). Succession planning in the third sector in New Zealand [Online]. *New Zealand Journal of Employment Relations, 37*(3), 34–49. Retrieved from http://search.proquest.com/docview/1413251527?accountid=458

Gay, L. R. (1996). *Educational research: Competencies for analysis and application* (4th ed.). Beverly Hills, CA: Sage.

Gay, L. R., & Airasian, P. (2000). *Educational research: Competencies for analysis and application* (6th ed.). New Jersey: Merrill.

Higgins, G. E., Ercikti, S., & Vito, G. F. (2013). Job satisfaction: Validating Dantzker's four-factor model using structural equation modeling. *Criminal Justice Studies, 26*(1), 19–29. doi:10.1080/1478601X.2012.731181

Hogue, H. B. (2012). *Congressional research service: Presidential transition act, provisions and funding, prepared for members and committees of Congress* (Order Code RS22979). Retrieved from file:///C:/UC%20Master/Road%20Files/RESEARCH/Command%20Transitions%20Article/Articles/CRS%202012%20Report%20RS22979.pdf

Horn, R. A. (2004). The new federal definition of educational research: Implications for educators. *The Teacher Educator, 39*(3), 196–212. Retrieved from ProQuest database, October 1, 2004.

Hughes, R. E., & Tomkiewicz, J. M. (1994). The academic organization's definition and assumptions: A basis for developing access to reasonable access to discipline actions [Electronic version]. *The International Journal of Educational Management, 8*(6), 4–8.

Jarrell, K. M., & Pewitt, K. C. (2007). Succession planning in government: Case study of a medium-sized city. *Review of Public Personnel Administration, 27*(3), 297–309. Retrieved from http://rop.sagepub.com/

Johnson, R. R. (2012). Police officer job satisfaction: A multidimensional analysis. *Police Quarterly, 15*(2), 157–176. Retrieved from http://pqx.sagepub.com/

Lee, V. E., Burkam, D. T., Ready, D. D., Honigman, J., & Meisels, S. J. (2006). Full-day versus half-day kindergarten: In which program do children learn more? [Electronic version]. *American Journal of Education, 112*(2), 163–208.

McNair, D. E. (2015). Deliberate disequilibrium: Preparing for a community college presidency. *Community College Review, 43*(1). Retrieved from http://crw.sagepub.com

Michelson, R. (2006). Preparing future leaders for tomorrow: Succession planning for police leadership. *Police Chief, 73*(6), 16–22. Retrieved from http://www.theiacp.org/

Miller, H. A., Mire, S., & Kim, B. (2009). Predictors of job satisfaction among police officers: Does personality matter? *Journal of Criminal Justice, 37*, 419–426. Retrieved from http://www.sciencedirect.com/science/journal/00472352

Neuman, W. L. (2003). *Social research methods: Qualitative and quantitative approaches* (5th ed.). Boston: Allyn and Bacon. Pendleton Act of 1883, Public Law § 16 (1883). Retrieved from http://www.ourdocuments.gov/doc.php?doc=48#

President Transition Act of 1963, Public Law § 88–277 (1964).

Presidential Transitions Effectiveness Act. Public Law § 100–398 (1988).

Presidential Transition Act of 2000. Public Law § 106–293 (2000).

Rothwell, W. J. (2010). *Effective succession planning: Ensuring leadership continuity and building talent from within*. New York: AMACOM.

Smith, S. (2008). *CRS report for congress: Presidential transitions, prepared for members and committees of congress* (Order Code RL30736). Retrieved from http://fas.org/sgp/crs/misc/RL30736.pdf

Su, S. H. (2006). Cultural differences in determining the ethical-perception and decision-making of future accounting professionals: A comparison between accounting students from Taiwan and the United States [Electronic version]. *Journal of American Academy of Business, 9*(1), 147–158.

The Public Health and Welfare: Bureau of Justice Statistics, 42 U.S.C. § 3732 (2006). U.S. Const. art. II, § 1–4.

U.S. Department of Justice, Office of Justice Programs, Bureau of Justice Statistics. (2011). *Census of state and local law enforcement agencies, 2008* (NCH Publication No. 233982). Retrieved from file:///C:/UC%20Master/Road%20Files/RESEARCH/Command%20Transitions%20Article/Articles/Census%20of%20State%20&%20Local%20LE%20Agencies%20BJS%20csllea08.pdf

U.S. Department of Justice, Bureau of Justice Statistics. (2011). *Law enforcement management and administrative statistics, 2007*. Ann Arbor, MI: Inter-university Consortium for Political and Social Research. Retrieved from http://www.icpsr.umich.edu/icpsrweb/ICPSR/studies/31161

U.S. General Services Administration, Office of Information and Regulatory Affairs, Office of Management and Budget, Executive Office of the President. (2012). *2012 LEMAS supporting statement, part a v2*. Retrieved from http://www.reginfo.gov/public/do/PRAViewDocument?ref_nbr=201209-1121-002

U.S. Department of Justice, Bureau of Justice Statistics. (2014). *Law enforcement*. Retrieved from http://www.bjs.gov/index.cfm?ty=tp&tid=7

Withrow, J. D. (2003). Succession planning: Reflecting on university police departments in Florida. *Campus Law Enforcement Journal, 33*(1), 12–16. Retrieved from http://search.proquest.com/docview/197899977?accountid=458

Appendix A
Survey Introductory Letter/Email

UTICA COLLEGE

1600 Burrstone Road
Utica, New York 13502
Phone—(315) 792-3246
jbrown@utica.edu

November 2014

Dear [redacted] Member:

You are receiving this email to participate in an important research initiative through the support of your [redacted] leadership. Effective transitions of power are essential to the smooth operation of any public administration organization, in particular a criminal justice agency. Prior research has shown generalized discussion surrounding agency succession planning. Transitions, however, are differentiated from succession planning within this research project, along with the associated attitudes and behaviors of those engaged in both behaviors. The problem is that no research has been conducted or discovered that addresses this critical element of organizational operations.

This research will address the problem by measuring satisfaction and preparedness of current/former criminal justice commanders regarding their transition experiences. By capturing these data it is hoped that we can further develop a command transitions matrix to allow agency leaders and policy makers within criminal justice and other public administration agencies and organizations to more effectively manage these heretofore seemingly ministerial transitions of power at all levels within the agency or organization; thus yielding a more satisfied, prepared, and ultimately more effective supervisor.

J.C. Brown et al., *Command Transitions in Public Administration*,
SpringerBriefs in Policing, DOI 10.1007/978-3-319-27844-5

We are asking you to participate in a very important research study that could help not only your agency or organization, but criminal justice agencies around the globe with future transitions of power at all levels. By agreeing to serve as one of two major New York State Associations of current and former criminal justice agency leaders, your association is committed to using the results of this research study in hopes of identifying any areas of concern and working to share the results to the wider criminal justice community. You are receiving this email for the study because you are either a current or former supervisor/leader in a criminal justice agency, and a member of this association.

The research study questionnaire link you are receiving is **voluntary** and will take you only approximately 10–15 min. to complete; using a SurveyMonkey® electronic platform to collect the data. You can be assured that if you respond to this research study that your response will remain confidential and anonymous. There is no place on the questionnaire for your name or other data to link you to the questionnaire you return. The only identifying information in the study will be aggregate demographic data that cannot be tied to you or your current/former agency/organization. Your name cannot be associated with your returned questionnaire and the results and the final report will only refer to the associations as association A and association B, located in New York State.

Refusal to participate will involve no known penalty to you or loss of benefits to which you may enjoy as a member of this association, or your agency/organization. You may discontinue participation at any time without any known penalty or loss of benefits, to which you may enjoy as a member of this association, or your agency/organization.

The data collected from this research study will be aggregated and shared with each association and the larger criminal justice community through various professional outlets such as journals and conferences. The raw data itself will be secured by the principal investigator in an encrypted, password protected file and only shared with the co-investigators involved in this research study. By submitting your survey you provide your informed consent and you waive no legal rights.

This research study has received approval from the Utica College Institutional Review Board (Dr. Robert Halliday, Chairman; 315-792-3122).

We would be pleased to answer any questions that you may have at this time regarding the research study. Please feel free to contact the principal investigator, Dr. James C. Brown, at any time should you have any questions or require any additional information. To begin the study, click here. If the link does not work, you may type in this address to your computer's browser: https://www.surveymonkey.com/s/commandtransitions. **Please look to complete the survey as soon as possible, but no later than Wednesday, November 26**.

Thank you in advance for your support of this important research study. All the best!

Sincerely,

Dr. James C. Brown, Principal Investigator
Professor of Practice—Criminal Justice
New York State [redacted]—Member

Raymond L. Philo, MPA, Co-Investigator
Professor of Practice—Economic Crime and Justice Studies
New York State [redacted]—Member

Anthony Callisto, Jr., MPA, Co-Investigator
Chief of Public Safety, Syracuse University
New York State [redacted]—Member

Appendix B
Survey Instrument

Criminal Justice Command Transition Satisfaction and Preparedness Survey (CJCTSPS).

An Organizational Readiness Matrix Tool.

Confidentiality and Anonymity

The information that you provide will remain strictly confidential and your anonymity is assured. There is no way to associate your answers with you or your agency.

Background

This Criminal Justice Command Transition Satisfaction and Preparedness Survey (CJCTSPS) has been designed to help policy makers within criminal justice and other public administration organizations measure their readiness for command transitions. By measuring self-reported supervisory personnel satisfaction and preparedness, coupled with evidence-based transitional best practices, criminal justice and other public administration policy makers will be better equipped to prepare their organizations to more effectively navigate these mission critical, but heretofore seemingly ministerial transitions of power at all levels of an organization.

The questionnaire is divided into three (3) key parts. The first section asks you general biographical data. Next, CJCTSPS asks you about your general perceptions toward your current/former organization and your specific career transition(s). Finally, you are asked to provide any additional qualitative/narrative details of your command transition experiences.

Instructions—How to Complete the Survey

1. Please answer all questions.
2. Completion of the survey should take approximately 10–15 min.

J.C. Brown et al., *Command Transitions in Public Administration*,
SpringerBriefs in Policing, DOI 10.1007/978-3-319-27844-5

3. Please give your first and natural answer; try not to dwell tc long on each response.
4. Please base your answers on your best recollection at the time you were actively engaged in transitioning between various roles within your current/former agency/agencies.

Section I—Biographical Data

Q1—I am currently

1. Retired
2. Active full-time (>35 h/week)
3. Active part-time (<20 h/week)

Q2—I am currently

1. Retired, former Commissioner/Superintendent
2. Retired, former Chief of Police
3. Retired, former Sheriff
4. Retired, former Assistant/Deputy Chief of Police/Assistant–Deputy Superintendent
5. Retired, former Undersheriff
6. Retired, former Commander/Major
7. Retired, former Chief Deputy
8. Retired, former Captain
9. Retired, former Lieutenant
10. Retired, former Sergeant
11. Retired, other supervisor/rank, please list________________________
12. Active, former Commissioner
13. Active, Chief of Police
14. Active, Sheriff
15. Active, Assistant/Deputy Chief of Police/Assistant–Deputy Superintendent
16. Active, Undersheriff
17. Active, Commander/Major
18. Active, Chief Deputy
19. Active, Captain
20. Active, Lieutenant
21. Active, Sergeant
22. Active, other supervisor/rank, please list________________________

Q3—In my most senior role during my career, I was/am responsible for supervising

1. 0–5 sworn and civilian personnel
2. 6–10 sworn and civilian personnel
3. 11–15 sworn and civilian personnel

4. 16–20 sworn and civilian personnel
5. 21–25 sworn and civilian personnel
6. 26–30 sworn and civilian personnel
7. 31–35 sworn and civilian personnel
8. 36–40 sworn and civilian personnel
9. 41–50 sworn and civilian personnel
10. 51–75 sworn and civilian personnel
11. 76–100 sworn and civilian personnel
12. 101–125 sworn and civilian personnel
13. 126–150 sworn and civilian personnel
14. 151–200 sworn and civilian personnel
15. 201–250 sworn and civilian personnel
16. 251–300 sworn and civilian personnel
17. 301–400 sworn and civilian personnel
18. 401–500 sworn and civilian personnel
19. >501 sworn and civilian personnel
20. If greater than 501, please list________

Q4—In your current/former position(s), how long did you/have you worked for your agency?

1. Less than 1 year
2. 1–2 years
3. 2–4 years
4. 4–6 years
5. 6–8 years
6. 8–10 years
7. 10–15 years
8. 15–20 years
9. 20–25 years
10. 25–30 years
11. >30 years
12. If >30 years, please list______

Q5—In my most senior current/former role

1. I occupy/occupied a civil service tested position (came from a civil service list); promoted from within the agency.
2. I occupy/occupied a civil service tested position (came from a civil service list); promoted from outside of the agency.
3. I was not a member of my current organization when I was appointed to my current/former leadership position.
4. I was a member of my current organization when I was appointed to my current/former leadership position.
5. I was not a member of my current organization when I was elected to my current/former leadership position.

6. I was a member of my current organization when I was elected to my current/former leadership position.

Q6—I am a

1. Male
2. Female

Q7—I am……years of age

1. 20–25
2. 26–30
3. 31–35
4. 36–40
5. 41–45
6. 46–50
7. 51–55
8. 56–60
9. 61–65
10. 66–70
11. 71–75
12. 76–80
13. If greater than 80, please list______

Q8—My marital status is

1. Married
2. Divorced
3. Widowed
4. Living with a partner
5. Single
6. Separated

Q9—If you are married/living with a partner, does he/she work?

1. Yes, full-time
2. No
3. Yes, part-time
4. No
5. Not applicable

Q10—Number of children less than 18 years of age

1. None
2. 1
3. 2
4. 3
5. 5
6. >5

Q11—Number of children greater than 18 years of age

1. None
2. 1
3. 2
4. 3
5. 5
6. >5

Q12—The highest level of education that I have completed is

1. General education degree (GED)
2. High-school diploma
3. Some college credits (no degree earned)
4. Associate's degree
5. Bachelor's degree
6. Master's degree
7. Doctoral degree

Q13—My race, according to the United States Census is

1. White
2. Black, African American, or Negro
3. Hispanic, Latino, or Spanish origin
4. American Indian or Alaska Native
5. Asian Indian
6. Chinese
7. Filipino
8. Other Asian
9. Japanese
10. Korean
11. Vietnamese
12. Native Hawaiian
13. Guamanian or Chamorro
14. Samoan
15. Other Pacific Islander
16. Other race

Section II—Perceptions of My Transition(s)

Over your career you have moved from an entry-level Police Officer/Deputy Sheriff to a first-line supervisor, and beyond. In some cases, you may have leaped multiple levels and were thrust into a senior supervisory role through appointment to a non-competitive position, or election. As you answer these questions, consider your level of satisfaction with the process/processes you encountered during these transitions, and your level of preparedness.

Q14—Please select one response for each statement below regarding your level of satisfaction with the process/processes encountered during your transitions between supervisory positions.

		Strongly disagree	Disagree	Slightly disagree	Slightly agree	Agree	Strongly agree
1	I knew what the requirements were for my most recent supervisory job prior to starting the assignment	☐	☐	☐	☐	☐	☐
2	I was provided with clear job expectations for my most recent supervisory job prior to starting the assignment	☐	☐	☐	☐	☐	☐
3	I am satisfied with the support I received from my agency when I was promoted to most recent supervisory job	☐	☐	☐	☐	☐	☐
4	There was a written policy/procedure that guided me as I undertook my most recent supervisory job	☐	☐	☐	☐	☐	☐
5	There was no orientation provided by my agency as I assumed my most recent supervisory job	☐	☐	☐	☐	☐	☐
6	There was no support provided to me as I assumed my most recent supervisory job	☐	☐	☐	☐	☐	☐
7	I am/was satisfied with the level of support I received from my agency as I assumed my most recent supervisory job	☐	☐	☐	☐	☐	☐
8	I was required to attend formal supervisory training outside of my agency as I assumed my most recent supervisory job	☐	☐	☐	☐	☐	☐

(continued)

		Strongly disagree	Disagree	Slightly disagree	Slightly agree	Agree	Strongly agree
9	I was required to attend formal supervisory training inside of my agency as I assumed my most recent supervisory job	☐	☐	☐	☐	☐	☐
10	I was supported by a formal transition team and/or mentor as I assumed my most recent supervisory job	☐	☐	☐	☐	☐	☐
11	I have primarily learned my supervisory skills through observation and my personal experiences	☐	☐	☐	☐	☐	☐
12	My job performance as a supervisor is (was, if retired/former) closely monitored by my supervisors	☐	☐	☐	☐	☐	☐
13	I feel/felt prepared as a supervisor in my most current job	☐	☐	☐	☐	☐	☐
14	I became a supervisor because of the better pay	☐	☐	☐	☐	☐	☐
15	I feel (felt, if retired/former) supported by my supervisors	☐	☐	☐	☐	☐	☐
16	I feel (felt, if retired/former) appreciated by my colleagues at my agency	☐	☐	☐	☐	☐	☐
17	I knew what was expected of me the first day I was a new supervisor	☐	☐	☐	☐	☐	☐
18	I had/have regular meetings with my supervisors as I assume/d my current (most recent, if retired/former) supervisory job	☐	☐	☐	☐	☐	☐

(continued)

		Strongly disagree	Disagree	Slightly disagree	Slightly agree	Agree	Strongly agree
19	I have/had received all of the tools I feel that I need to perform my most recent supervisory job	☐	☐	☐	☐	☐	☐
20	I feel (felt, if retired/former) supported/backed by my supervisors when I make/made a decision	☐	☐	☐	☐	☐	☐
21	I am glad that I am (was, if retired/former) a criminal justice supervisor	☐	☐	☐	☐	☐	☐

Section III—Narrative Responses

Q15—Is there any information from the above questions/statements that you would like to further explain? If so, please identify the question and provide your comments.

Q16—Is there anything else that you would like to add regarding your current/past experiences as you transitioned between entry-level and various supervisory positions? If so, please add them below:

Q17—Were there any books or other publications that were provided/ recommended to you as you assumed your most current supervisory role? If yes, please name/discuss them.

Q18—Were there any professional organizations that were required for you to joint or recommended to you as you assumed your most current supervisory role? If yes, please name or discuss them.

Q19—Please add any other comments here:

Thank you for your participation in this important research.

If you are interested in receiving a copy of the findings of this research, or have any questions, please contact the principal researcher, Dr. James C. Brown, Utica College, 1600 Burrstone Road, Utica, New York 13502; email: jbrown@utica.edu. Phone: (315) 792-3246.

Appendix C
Variable Frequency Distribution Histogram(S)

See Figs. 1, 2, 3, 4, 5, 6, 7, 8, 9, 10 and 11.

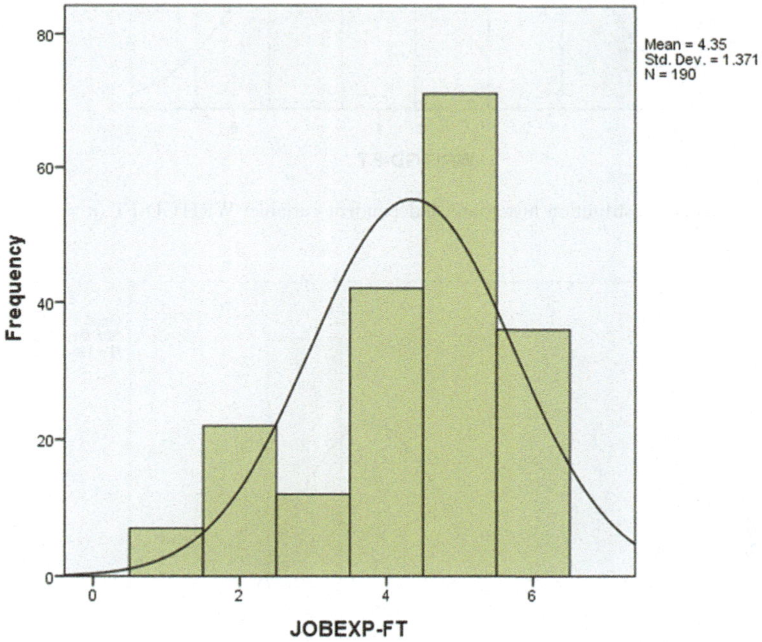

Fig. 1 Frequency distribution histogram, independent variable; JOBEXP-FT (n = 190)

J.C. Brown et al., *Command Transitions in Public Administration*,
SpringerBriefs in Policing, DOI 10.1007/978-3-319-27844-5

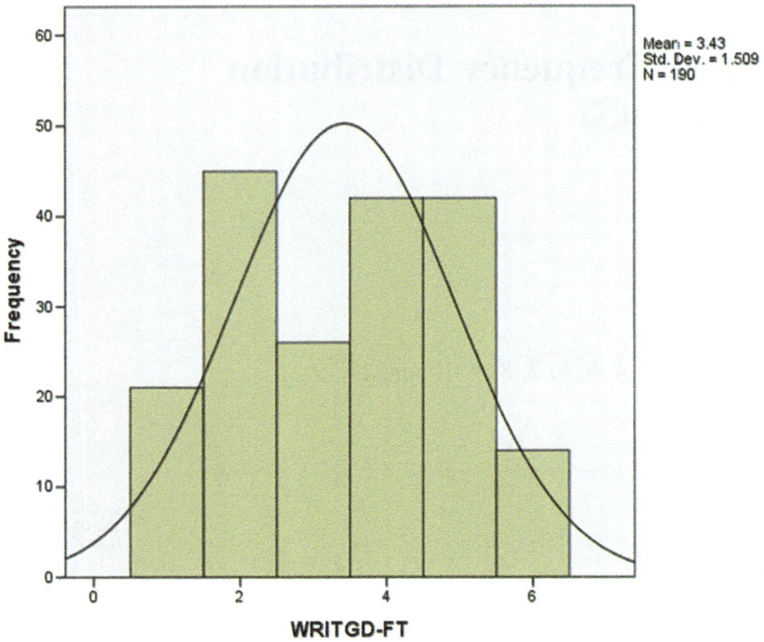

Fig. 2 Frequency distribution histogram, independent variable; WRITGD-FT (n = 190)

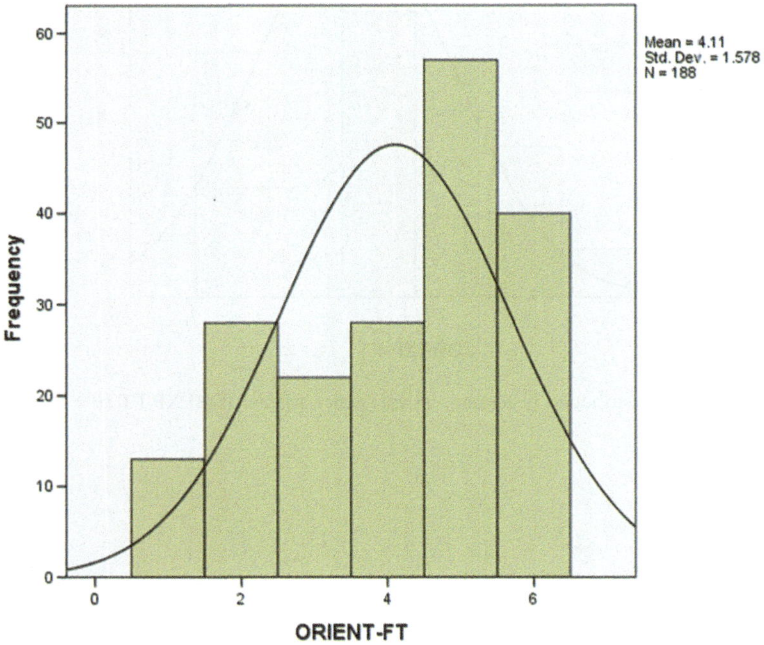

Fig. 3 Frequency distribution histogram, independent variable; ORIENT-FT (n = 188)

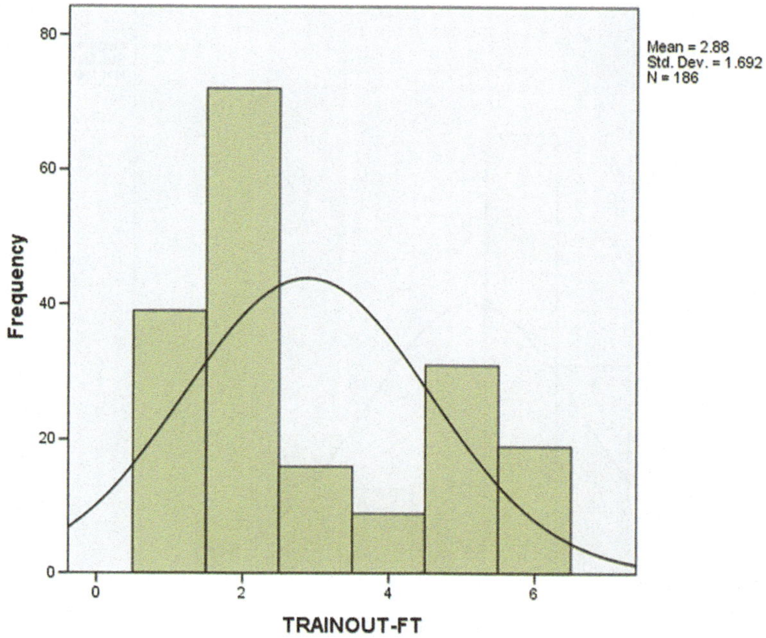

Fig. 4 Frequency distribution histogram, independent variable; TRAINOUT-FT (n = 186)

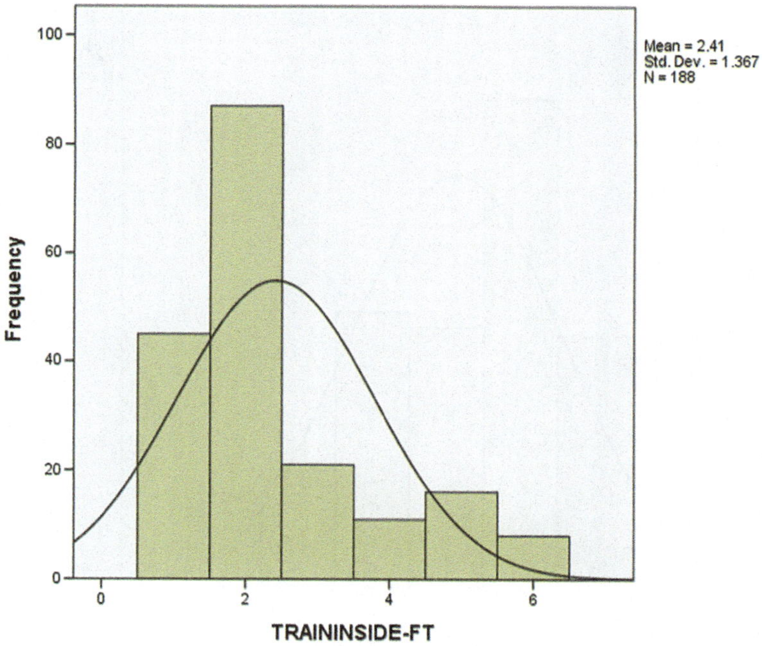

Fig. 5 Frequency distribution histogram, independent variable; TRAININSIDE-FT (n = 188)

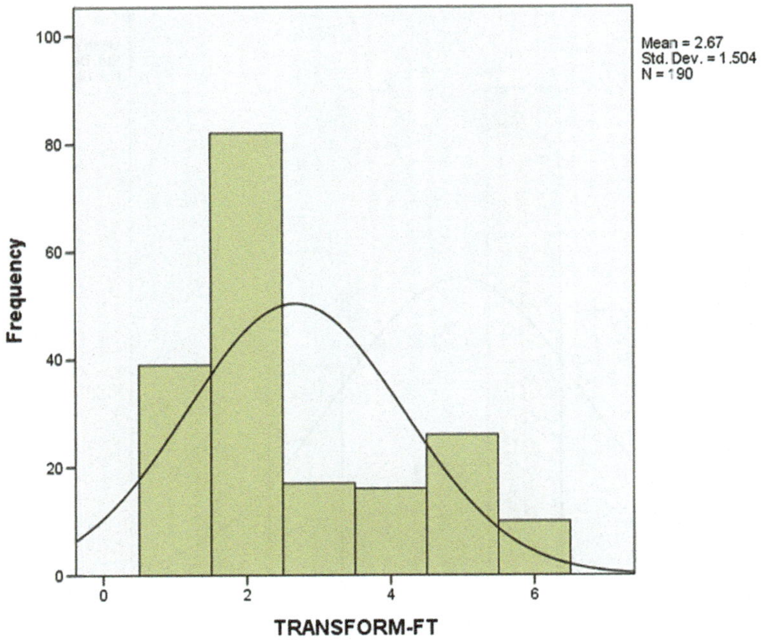

Fig. 6 Frequency distribution histogram, independent variable; TRANSFORM-FT (n = 190)

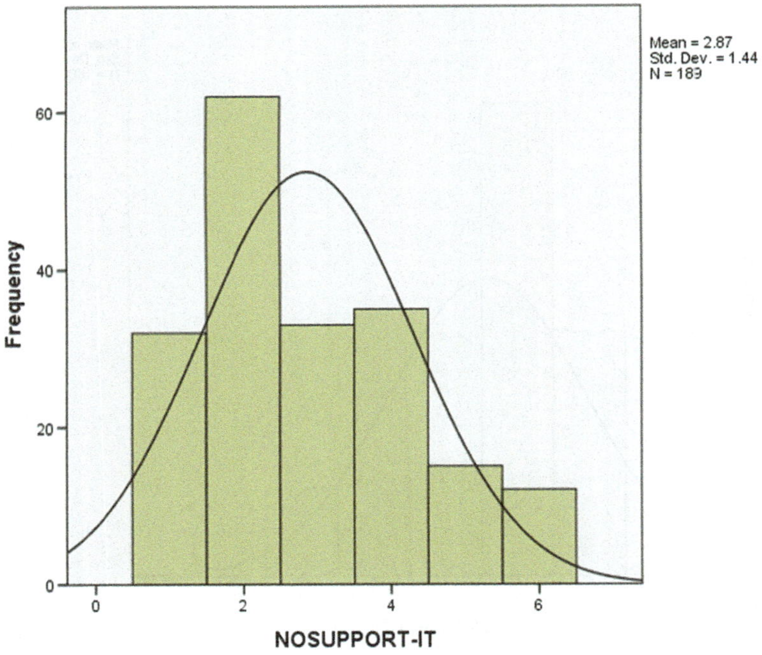

Fig. 7 Frequency distribution histogram, independent variable; NOSUPPORT-IT (n = 189)

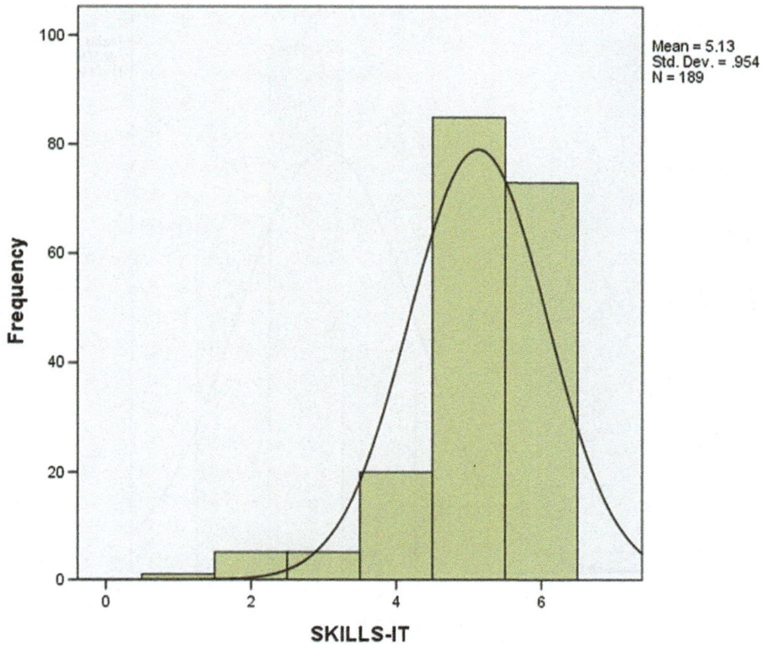

Fig. 8 Frequency distribution histogram, independent variable; SKILLS-IT (n = 189)

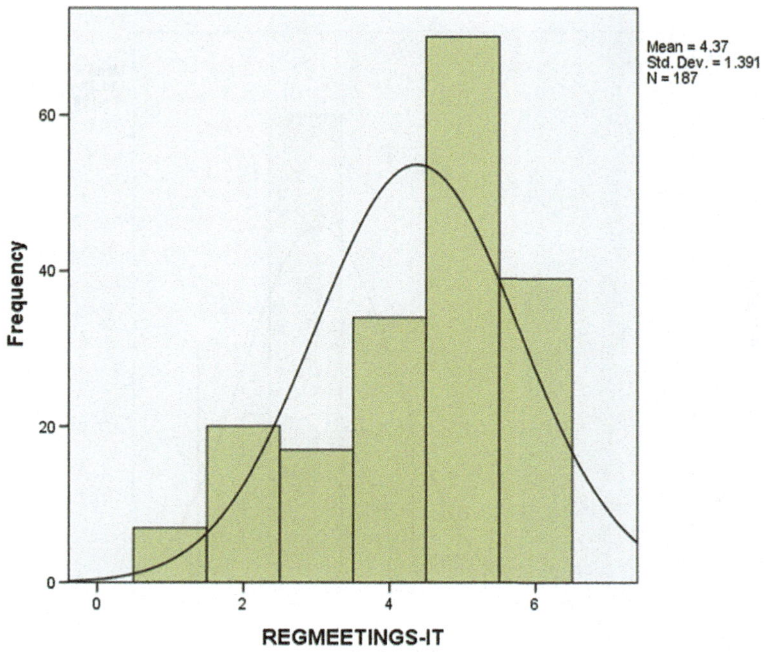

Fig. 9 Frequency distribution histogram, independent variable; REGMEETINGS-IT (n = 187)

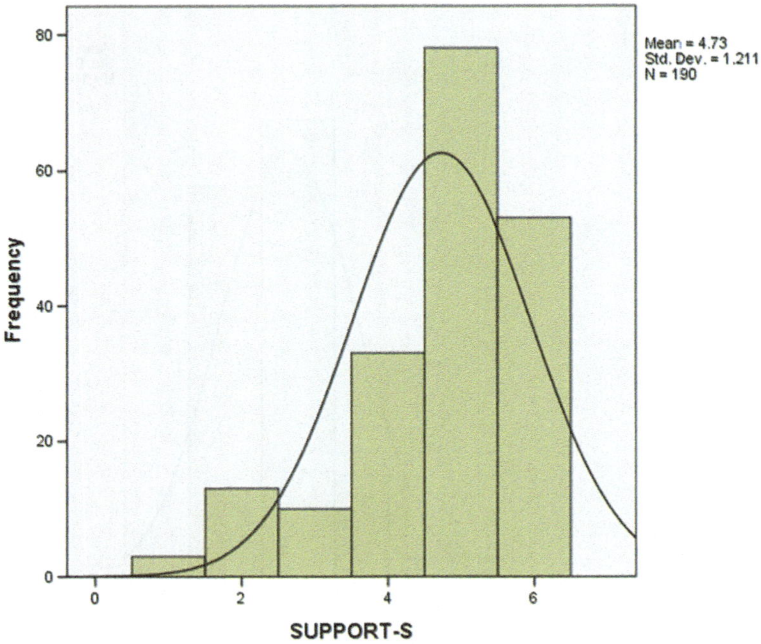

Fig. 10 Frequency distribution histogram, dependent variable representing satisfaction; SUPPORT-S (n = 190)

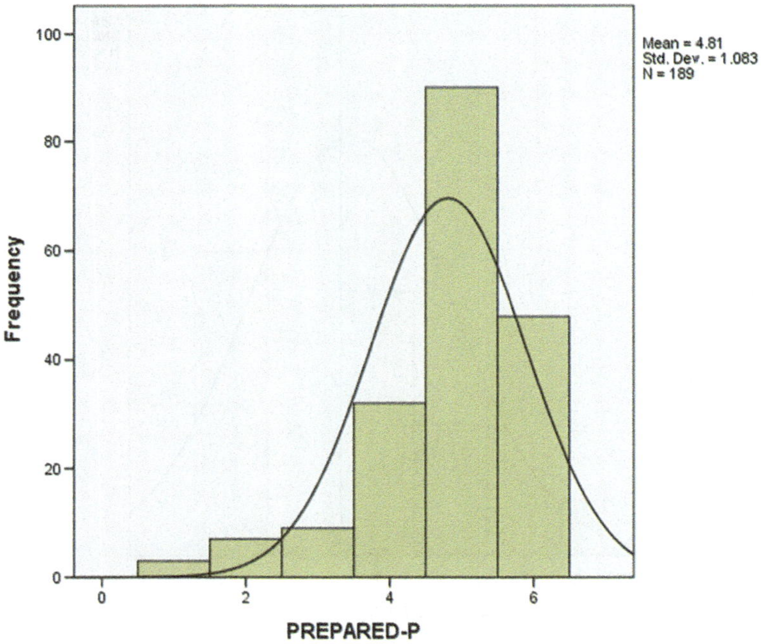

Fig. 11 Frequency distribution histogram, dependent variable representing preparedness; PREPARED-P (n = 189)

Appendix D
Select Qualitative Response Data[1]

Question 15: Is there any information from the above questions/statements that you would like to further explain? If so, please identify the question and provide your comments.

1. There is training for the first-line supervisors and then it falls short—Union Labor relations and Negotiations—dealing with manpower issues and grievances has been a learning experience with little guidance from training.
2. Although my agency does a good job of supporting its subordinates to execute their jobs it does a poor job of developing the staff as a whole. At one time supervisors were required to attend a certified one/two week supervisor academy. However, that no longer exists. We rely strictly on the individual's personal competence, capability, education, experience, and willingness for self-development. Although this is something we look for in our staff in order to become supervisors, we strongly lack the institutional fortitude to develop them. It is not that we don't have the capability as a Department, just the will. The three legs of development, experiential, personal, and institutional, are there in order to grow our future leaders. We severely lack in the institutional. Our experiential is stunted due in large part to the civil service laws and the agency does not promote any kind of personal growth. We are currently experiencing an arrested development.
3. It was a culmination of training and experience from all of my supervisory positions assumed along the path until being appointed to Undersheriff that prepared me for the role. My college education was also critically important to my success.
4. There was no on-the-job supervisory training provided after being promoted.
5. The experience that I have accrued in my first ten years as a corrections officer has allowed me to make sound decisions as a supervisor. I work very closely with my subordinates and will continue to do so to help them achieve a higher level of professionalism.
6. I was promoted to the Chief of Police position from patrol officer. Our department had been without a chief for months and the village I work for was

[1]Presented in their entirety; not edited for grammatical/mechanical errors only.

J.C. Brown et al., *Command Transitions in Public Administration*,
SpringerBriefs in Policing, DOI 10.1007/978-3-319-27844-5

recovering from a devastating flood. The previous chief left abruptly, so there was no "transition."

7. I have transferred from my local department to another department within the statewide agency. The similarities and differences can be staggering to a new supervisor.
8. I made/make the effort to seek outside training to better myself as a supervisor on my own volition.
9. I stepped in as chief after the department had prior chief out for almost a year. There was no transition from prior chief.
10. Some of my supervisors are supportive. Others are a large part of the problems. Issues stem from policies being "reinterpreted" to fit the need of the facility at the time. Officers and first-line supervisors are then held accountable for not knowing the policies and procedures. Staff is not free to manage their housing units because they are not confident that they will make the correct decision for that day or situation.
11. Most individuals in our supervisory position do not take the position for the money. We are looking to make positive change.
12. I was promoted to captain after the pervious captain retired. I received no orientation or transition period to what the job entailed, except for "looking up" as a patrol lieutenant. Both the Sheriff and the Undersheriff were also new to their positions. I learned as I went along.
13. I was not required to attend supervisory training outside my agency but chose to do so. National Sheriff's Institute.
14. My former employer did not support its supervisors nor encourage them. This actually provided me with a better understanding of the importance of this when I assumed my new role.
15. I was not compelled to attend any internal or external training but rather provided financial resources to attend training and conferences in support of my new position. I have regularly attended the NYSACOP conference and IACP conference since taking office in 2006.
16. There was not a lot of tasks required by the Board who hired me.
17. Need to memorialize all procedures and protocols.
18. I was the first Chief of a newly formed Police Department and therefore had no formal guidance.
19. Prepromotional training is difficult. Preparing for the next level requires investment in personnel who may or may not take and/or pass a civil service test. Many agencies simply cannot pay to train someone until after the promotion.
20. I encountered what happens in most small towns, which is very little transition and preparation. The hardest part nobody could have prepared me for was being friends with my subordinates and still being their boss.

Question 16: Is there anything else that you would like to add regarding your current/past experiences as you transitioned between entry-level and various supervisory positions? If so, please add them below:

1. Command-level support is critical for subordinates
2. Any and all supervisory training is appreciated. Sometimes it is assumed that we are highly educated in supervisory/leadership functions due to the rank we attained.
3. Promoted in SP from Trooper to Investigator, Sr. Investigator, Lieutenant, and Captain. Attended SP provided training at each level of promotion along with in service training. Forced to retire due to age and trained for DOJ 4 years. Became Undersheriff after a change in Sheriff's, transition between Sheriff's was not so smooth. Former employment helped prepare me for my current position. This study is much needed and appreciated for those that follow!
4. I was given some informal supervisor training by being assigned to work with another supervisor before I was promoted. That is not the norm. Most people promoted are promoted and thrown to the wolves without any formal or informal training.
5. The field training for supervisors and commanders is ineffectual and needs to be greatly improved upon. There is a lack of command emphasis on the process which makes it an almost "pencil whipping" process.
6. I took over an office that was mismanaged for years and so had to teach myself and rely of my peers from other departments to find my way.
7. First-line supervision receives the most training in supervision and decreases as the individual ascends the ranks.
8. I believe that more classes are needed for members that are moving into supervisory positions. Focus needs to be on such topics as conducting internal investigations and criminal investigations on members, roles of supervisors and the effects of being a Supervisor.
9. I have been attending classes as time has allowed. I did not get support from the only Sergeant in the department but the officers working for me were and still are very supportive. I have had a continual battle with the Village Board of Trustees on everything from my pay (12,000 less than my predecessor) to hiring new officers and equipment purchases.
10. Very little if no transition training for any position. Before retiring a new chief, former-state Trooper Sergeant, was hired and there was no training or transition.
11. The Supervisor should become familiar with the union contract(s), agency policy/procedures, and budget as soon as possible.
12. There was a COC-sponsored Supervisory training that did not provide much guidance. I also had a 2 week FTO period with in my facility. This was more helpful but could have been improved on. Most of my training has been "learn as you go."
13. Very supportive in current position. In the PD it was learn by trial and error.
14. It is difficult replacing a prior supervisor who "let things go." I met with some resistance due to wanting things done correctly rather than overlooking them.

15. Transitional training for each supervisory level.
16. As a Sheriff, there should be minimum requirements to be a candidate for Sheriff!
17. As I moved thru many ranks, I had very little training for the new position.
18. There needs to be a better transition framework. There also needs to be a level of training from DCJS for things such as FOIL, budgeting, labor issues, personnel issues.
19. At the executive level, if you do a good job in one spot, it is assumed you will do well in others. There is no training and very little mentoring for executives in my agency.
20. Government as a whole does a poor job in the transition from line officer as you go through the ranks. I personally got most of my training by continued education and self-taught with reading books.
21. Originally a Deputy Sheriff, promoted to Detective, promoted to Det. Sgt., then promoted to Chief Deputy via C.S. exam result, and then promoted to Sheriff.
22. You may think you know the next position, but you really do not.
23. The most significant transition experiences were through one on one mentoring that I sought out.
24. I have enhanced my supervisory ability over the years by attending excellent supervisory schools.
25. I was a mayoral appointment but worked for a municipality that supported its Police Department. I was able to garner the support of even the political opposition.
26. Keep your friends close and your enemies closer.
27. Police leaders must be exposed to learning opportunities outside their own agencies. Taking what they learn from college courses, leadership and management seminars and books, etc., and applying them to their work will create the most beneficial learning opportunities for them to become more effective. A good mentor can facilitate this process.

Question 17: Were there any books or other publications that were provided/recommended to you as you assumed your most current supervisory role? If yes, please name/discuss them

Answer options	Response percentage	Response count
Yes	21.0	35
No	79.0	132

1. Police Chief magazine.
2. Some leadership books but I don't recall the titles.
3. Police Supervision and Manual for Police.
4. Police Tutorial service is a great resource for civil service test taking preparation. The FBI National Academy also provided excellent training for those who lead.

5. Supervising for success.
6. No books were recommended when going through the supervisor or commander field training program.
7. County Sheriff America's Last Hope—written by Sheriff Richard Mack **This was given to me by my Sheriff at time I was appointed.
8. I requested several books on leadership and management that were approved for purchase. Our Administrator commented "You can read all the books you want on leadership. That won't make you a good supervisor" during a Sergeant's Meeting just after receiving the books.
9. IACP Police Chief Desk Reference
10. Leadership Challenge by Kouzes and Posner—Give me the knowledge of the difference between a leader and a boss. Encouraged me to think outside of the normal box, support my members and listen and use their input. Sun Tzu for Success by Gerald Michaelson—Ideals on how to deal with everyday challenges and move ahead to accomplish goals.
11. Delattre—Character in Cops.
12. Police Supervision by Innone.
13. Movie "Glory" from leadership styles I have read the business or management books for Richard Marcinko, and "police liability" by Dennis Payne and Police Leadership by Haberfield
14. Grossman all his books
15. I did (and still do) a lot of research to such on my own and have shared what I learned with my subordinate supervisors. Some in turn have done their own research and share it with me. Together we are attempting to change the culture of leadership within our organization.
16. I researched my self.
17. Emotional Intelligence Managing Police Discipline Labor and Employment Law.
18. Policy and Procedure Manual.
19. Too numerous to mention from National Institute of Corrections, College Classes, etc.
20. None were provided, I sought several books, including manual for NYS police and Ionnones police manual.
21. IACP Chiefs Desktop Manual.
22. Challenging the Law Enforcement Organization, by Jack Enter, Ph.D.
23. The Road Less Traveled regarding personal growth. Good to Great by Jim Collins. Strengths Based Leadership by Tom Rath and Barry Conchie. Self-Leadership and the One Minute Manager. Make Today Count by John Maxwell. The Top Ten Mistakes Leader Make by Hans Finzel.
24. Not for this office, but as a first-line supervisor Iannone's "Supervision of Police Personnel" and as a training director "On Killing" by Lt Col Dave Grossman.
25. Challenging the Law Enforcement Organization—Proactive Leadership Strategies by Dr. Jack Enter.

26. Rules, regulations, policy, and procedures.
27. I have attended and graduated various professional programs such as the FBI Academy, the NYS Law Enforcement Executive Institute, and less lengthy programs such as Ethical Awareness Moderator, LEEDS Program and instructor Development. Every academic experience I've had has contributed greatly to my personal and professional development and I've taken at least some small thing from each, made it my own and put it into practice in my daily job responsibilities. If there is one source for leadership principles I would cite "Lincoln on Leadership."
28. Books on police supervision, don't recall the names. Attended a few classes and seminars on leadership and supervision presented by the FBI and different New York State academies.
29. Municipal Police Management—excellent text.
30. Ianonne's "Supervision of Police Personnel."
31. IACP Model policies IACP Chief's Manual NYS DCJS updates and memos IACP Chief's magazine Federal Government resources A variety of books dealing with management and supervision in law enforcement and in general outside of law enforcement.
32. N. Iannone's theory of police supervision.
33. Department Regulations and Accreditation Standards.
34. No one ever recommended any books to me during my police career. However, I have found these to be beneficial, "Challenging the Law Enforcement Organization" by Dr. Jack Enter, "Emotional Survival for Law Enforcement" by Dr. Kevin Gilmartin, "Supervision of Police Personnel" by Iannonne, "The Leadership Challenge" by Kousez and Posner, "Good to Great" and "How the Mighty Fall" by Jim Collins, and "Anyway: The Paradoxical Commandments" by Dr. Kent Keith.
35. Police Chief 101 (Gerald W. Garner).

Question 18: Were there any professional organizations that were required for you to join or recommended to you as you assumed your most current supervisory role? If yes, please name or discuss them

Answer options	Response percentage	Response count
Yes	45.4	79
No	54.6	95

1. Professional organizations were neither required nor recommended. I was however a member of the local County and CNY Chief's associations. There are times as chief that you feel you are on an island dealing with issues that no one else understands. But at these associations you quickly learn that there are other Chiefs who are dealing with similar issues and they are ready, willing and able to assist and do so graciously and openly. I would STRONGLY recommend to any new chief to join such organizations.

2. American Jail Association.
3. New York State Sheriff's Association *This organization has proven very valuable to me and my role through their trainings and collaboration with peers across the state. Great source of information sharing.
4. IACP NYSACOP Westchester County Chiefs of Police Assoc. None were required but I joined them all.
5. IACP, NYSACOP, PERF.
6. NYS Association of Chief of Police NY Police Chief's Benevolent Association.
7. Recommended NYS Sheriff's Association American Correctional Association (ACA) American Jail Association (AJA) Was a member of various Training Organizations Prior to employment: Empire State Law Enforcement Training Network NYS Trainers Association.
8. Not required but joined The American Correctional Association.
9. The New York State Sheriff's Association and the National Sheriff's Association.
10. New York State Sheriff's Association and the Nation Sheriff's Association have both been helpful in the transition and also over the last 7 years in my position as Sheriff.
11. New York State Sheriff's Association New York State Association of Chiefs of Police International Association of Chiefs of Police American Jail Association.
12. NYS Sheriffs Association, I Recommend anyone new to any agency or supervisory role join any organizations related to that agency or role played.
13. Attend the FBI National Academy. Attend the National Sheriffs' Institute.
14. I was recommended to join the New York State Chief's and the Northeastern Chief's of Police by fellow Chief's, not by my organization. The training, networking, and comradery received from these organizations was without question, the most significant impact on my transition and learning professional standards of the job. The staff, officers and members of the organizations were extremely inclusive and always just a phone call or email away.
15. International Association of Chiefs of Police New York State Association of Chiefs of Police Central new York Association of Chief of Police Onondaga County Chapter, Chief of Police Association International Association of Campus Law Enforcement Administrators.

Question 19: Please add other comments here:

1. I am encouraged by the offering of this survey. There should be better training for transitioning to supervisory roles. This should include on-the-job training with experienced supervisors.
2. Most new Chief's 20 years ago and before felt a part of a group with purpose that was respected and appreciated in this state and the recent decision by the State of NY to include the 207 m—Police Chief's bill in with the 2 % tax cap relief legislation was a slap to all Chief's statewide which was one of the few protections for the Chief who are not a member of the PBA unions? That was a blow to all Chief's and any member that wants to be a Chief in the future.

3. I'm hard on my Department because I see the great potential we have. Our failure to formalize the development of our staff shows in our mediocre productivity and lack of pride by many in the rank and file. I've made this known to my executive staff on numerous occasions and will continue to make those recommendations while I am still on active status. I will also develop those who I directly supervise and attempt to influence those I don't. However, it does feel like an uphill battle at times when the administration does not place command emphasis on development.
4. It is important to recognize that everyone learns in their own ways and that there is no one right way. Succession planning is important from the earliest stages. I believe new supervisors of today should be molded for higher positions of tomorrow. Passing the history and telling stories is an important component of teaching leadership within an organization.
5. In our department, as a supervisor is it very uncommon to get praise for the good things that we accomplish. Overall there has not been a lot of support from our superiors.
6. Other Chiefs and ranked Officers from other departments are my greatest asset.
7. Most "learning" was done by experience. The benefit of belonging to associations such as the IACP, state, and local ones as well which allow us to get training and interface w/peers.
8. No matter how long you are in the job, you need to constantly refresh and engage.
9. Staying current and analyzing your organizations health internally and with the community you serve is one of the major rolls for a Chief.
10. I was a graduate of the FBI National Academy 17 years before I became Chief. What I learned during those 11 weeks helped me tremendously.

Index

J.C. Brown et al., *Command Transitions in Public Administration*,
SpringerBriefs in Policing, DOI 10.1007/978-3-319-27844-5

The manufacturer's authorised representative in the EU is Springer Nature Customer Service Centre GmbH, Europaplatz 3, 69115 Heidelberg, Germany. If you have any concerns regarding our products, please contact ProductSafety@springernature.com

Printed and bound by CPI Group (UK) Ltd, Croydon, CR0 4YY
30/09/2026
02225575-0001